The Sale Ready Company

ENDORSEMENTS

"Josh is one of those people who usually thinks differently about the process of creating economically and sustainable businesses. In this book, you'll learn why sale ready is a term you need to learn to love and adopt for your company.

"Josh has spoken to our Profit First community, and he had our group thinking differently about their businesses and what they needed to do for personal and professional success."

—Mike Michalowicz
Author, *Profit First* and *Fix this Next*

"Josh has helped me think through many of the issues revealed in the book, and my business is better (and more profitable) for it. Even if you're not thinking about selling your company, this book will help you understand why having a sale ready company lets you enjoy your business more than you ever thought possible while also making more money than you ever thought possible."

—Michael Port, CEO, Heroic Public Speaking
New York Times and *Wall Street Journal*
Bestselling Author of 8 Books

"Josh Patrick is somebody I turn to when I need to understand complex issues. He makes them simple and easy to understand.

"Over the years, I've had the pleasure of getting to know Josh as a linchpin of—and unique voice in—the Book Yourself Solid® community. He's presented several times to our group and always brings new and fresh ideas to our members, who appreciate his expertise and approach.

"In this book, he reminds us how important a sale-ready company is and how creating one gives owners options they would never normally have. I would recommend you take the time to let Josh explain why 'sale ready' is so important and what you can do to make your company one that others will be hungry to own."

—Matthew Kimberley, Head of
Book Yourself Solid® Worldwide

"It takes one to know one; business owners have many shared experiences. It takes a unique business owner and consultant to break through the complexities and individual nuances to name and give a clear, practical process for managing these challenges.

"Great solutions, sage understanding, and an easy read; just what we expect from Josh Patrick."

—Susan Bradley, Founder
Financial Transitionist Institute
and Sudden Money Institute

"Josh is one of the people I go to when I have a thorny business issue to discuss. He covers many of them in this book. You'll learn why 'sale ready' is something you need to do. It'll make your life and company so much better."

—Walt Hampton, J.D.
Bestselling Author of *The Power Principles of Time Mastery: Do Less, Make More, Have Fun*

"Josh is one of those rare business advisors who understands success is about more than the money. In his newest book, we watch the journey of the Aardvark family struggling with some very real issues families face when attempting to transition their business to the next generation.

"There's a good chance you're going to recognize your family and business as you read this book. You'll walk away knowing why 'sale ready' is a crucial activity in business success."

—Courtney Pullen, President
The Pullen Consulting Group

"I've been in the succession planning space for private business owners for over fifty years. Too often I've seen explanations that are long and complicated.

"Josh's eight-step sale ready process is easy to understand, and having it told as a story makes it memorable as well. Read this book and apply the principles in it. You'll be better for it."

—Peter Christman, Co-Founder,
Exit Planning Institute

"Josh has worked with our company on and off for years. We love to have him come in when we need to have a view from the balcony when we want to focus on big strategic issues our company faces.

"In this book, he does the same for the Aardvark family. I saw many of the issues in the book as ones we've faced in our company. It's a real-world story with real-world problems."

—Peter Asch, CEO and Chairman,
Twincraft Skincare

"I don't think anyone I know understands family business the way Josh does. He knows the people, how they think, and what they want like they're part of his own family. This book makes them come to life, recognizes their humanity with all of its thorns, and teaches us all many valuable lessons."

—Randy Fox, Principal, Two Hawks Consulting

"When it comes to generational business transfer, Josh is THE guy. Having worked with him personally on the transfer of my own family's business from one generation to the next, I feel confident saying that his wisdom and guidance have been absolutely crucial to our process. We also developed a personal relationship along the way that I greatly value. If you are looking to transfer your business or just love learning about business, then this book is a MUST read."

—Seth Frumkin, Vice President, Kipcon Engineering
and Next Generation Owner

"In *The Sale Ready Company*, Aaron's courage to walk alongside people in a nurturing way powerfully permits them to look at realities they cannot or will not easily entertain. This book works generatively from the contextual level (rather than exclusively in the content) to explore existing perspectives—resulting in the rare combination of a more accurate and comprehensive understanding while taking action as well."

—Joel Marquardt, President, Twincraft Skincare

"In *The Sale Ready Company*, Josh Patrick has identified not only a process for getting your business ready for sale, but he also addresses the emotional needs of all the people involved in marketing a small business.

"There have been many of these same issues involved in dealing with my own succession plan—from family dynamics, preparing the business to be sold, partners of different ages, and addressing what the business needs are to grow to finance a successful retirement. Possibly the most poignant aspect of this process was getting the business owner to understand the next chapter. Is the spouse prepared for their time to be impeached by the retiring business owner; is the retiring business owner prepared to let go? All of this is addressed in an engaging manner that really points out that outside counsel is essential."

—Ron Wilkinson, CFP® CeFT®
Principal, Security First Advisors

The SALE READY COMPANY

What It Takes to Create a Business
SOMEONE ELSE WOULD WANT TO OWN,
Even If You Have No Intention of Selling

JOSH PATRICK

NEW YORK

LONDON • NASHVILLE • MELBOURNE • VANCOUVER

The SALE READY COMPANY

What It Takes to Create a Business Someone Would Want to Own, Even if Your Have No Intention of Selling

Published in New York, New York, by Morgan James Publishing. Morgan James is a trademark of Morgan James, LLC. www.MorganJamesPublishing.com

ISBN 9781631953293 paperback
ISBN 9781631953309 eBook
Library of Congress Control Number: 2020946224

Cover and Interior Design by:
Chris Treccani
www.3dogcreative.net

Morgan James is a proud partner of Habitat for Humanity Peninsula and Greater Williamsburg. Partners in building since 2006.

Get involved today! Visit
MorganJamesPublishing.com/giving-back

This book is dedicated to my favorite uncle, George Patrick, my biggest supporter on this book and in life.

TABLE OF CONTENTS

FOREWORD

If your first thought when you received this book was, "Oh no! Not another book on family business planning!" then join the club.

I've received more than my share of these books (and written a few), but when I saw that Josh Patrick was the author, I knew this book would be different from the others. Different because Josh is different—but different in a good way.

I know Josh to be a straight shooter who has made it his mission to help his business-owner clients benefit from their lives' work. Based on a years-long friendship and working as colleagues, I can tell you that Josh doesn't mince words or pull his punches. You will find his candor to be refreshing as you read about one family—the Aardvarks—in its quest to transfer business ownership within the family. (Only Josh would have chosen "Aardvark" as the name for the central characters in his saga. Perhaps it's an old family name because, from some angles, I can see the resemblance.)

As do most owners in family business transfers, the Aardvarks experience a host of family disputes and disagreements, some of which are satisfactorily resolved, others not so much. That's the realistic outcome of most family business transfer planning—not every family member ends up satisfied. Josh describes the factors that owners must consider as they make the tough decisions and how skilled advisors can help them.

What's strikingly different about this book, however, is that Josh focuses on the changing thoughts, feelings, and perspectives that both owners-parents *and their children* experience in deciding whether, and how, to transfer ownership of a family-owned business. In addition, Josh uses the Aardvarks to illustrate some of the most common concerns of important employees and how transition can affect the growth and stability of a business.

No book about business transfers would be complete without mention of the issues and challenges (e.g., tax strategies, business financial strengths and weaknesses) that most owners face when transferring a business, but I commend Josh for shining a spotlight on the feelings, family relationships, and emotions that drive owners to make ownership decisions and occasionally reverse course.

Whether you are a business owner or someone who works with owners, this book will give you rare insight into how families make decisions (or not). The Aardvark's advisor (Aaron) illustrates the central role that an advisor experienced in exit planning can play in keeping the transfer process moving forward. Advisors like Aaron know how to maintain momentum while managing the often-competing interests of children, employees, and spouses.

There is much advisors can learn from Aaron about quarterbacking a complex process and much owners can learn from John Aardvark when they assume they are the only ones overwhelmed by the challenges that the transfer of their businesses presents.

As you read on, advisors: Pay attention! Owners: Prepare to meet a close relative of the person you see in the mirror every morning. When you finish this book, advisors and owners will have a game plan for moving forward.

—John Brown
Founder, Business Enterprise Institute

A NOTE FROM THE AUTHOR

Welcome to the world of the Aardvarks. Like many privately held companies, there are challenges and even some dysfunctions in the family and the business.

You're going to learn what it takes to make the first steps toward creating a business that can last for one hundred years. The first, and maybe most difficult, step is to do the first transition to the next owners.

You'll also learn it's not the transition that's the hard part. You'll learn the plan will determine the success or failure of this transition. Understanding what the family wants to do, and why it's important, is the key.

You'll find lots of strategies that you can apply to your own business, even if you have no interest in selling. You'll find the Aardvarks are going to take steps that will create a sale ready company, even if they have no immediate interest in selling.

Too often I have business owners tell me they aren't interested in selling their company, so there is no reason for them to create a sale ready company. This is a huge mistake because a sale ready company allows you, as the owner, to have more options in what you can do with your business.

Although John Aardvark is not interested in selling today, he knows he needs to position the company for the next generation of ownership. He isn't sure what he needs to do or why he even wants to plan for the next step.

Confused, John calls his consultant Aaron to have a conversation. This conversation leads both John and Aardvark Manufacturing on the road to preparing for the next generation of owners, even though the transfer won't start for a few years.

Join us as we learn how John solves his dilemmas. I bet you'll find at least some similarities in your company and even some of the same challenges and problems that Aardvark has.

I hope you enjoy reading this book as much as I've enjoyed writing it.

—Josh Patrick
Hinesburg, Vermont

CHAPTER 1

Introduction

John Aardvark is sitting at his desk, looking out the window. He sighs. Over the past four years, his business has doubled; this after ten years of stagnation. He's put two additions onto his building, and his company has hired forty new people. This is a lot of growth. Yet it confuses him that his business isn't financially more successful. Shouldn't all of this growth mean he's making more money and enjoying his time more? And why isn't he happier?

John has spent a lot of time and energy learning how to delegate, stay out of the way, and stop being a helicopter manager. He has some great people, including Janice Moreway, his Chief Operating Officer or, as he likes to say, his integrator.

Janice is the one who brought in a new plant manager, George Johnson, who is also doing great work. The only challenge is that George and John's son, Adam, are always at each other's throats. If Adam weren't his son, John would have taken him out of the key position of maintenance supervisor long ago. In fact, if his wife, Ann, weren't so adamant about Adam staying with the company, John would fire him.

John is thinking about Aaron, the consultant, and the work he did with the company. As much as John hates to admit it, Aaron brings a lot of sorely needed organization, focus, and change. It's no coincidence that the serious growth at Aardvark started right after their first collaboration.

John keeps asking himself… why is he so unhappy?

Once again John feels stuck. Six years ago, he wanted to throw in the towel. That's when he'd ended up at a Chamber of Commerce mixer and was introduced to Aaron.

Now he is getting pressure from his daughter, Alicia, to put together a real succession plan. Although the business is growing like crazy and is supposedly making much more money, there is no excess cash. On top of that, he doesn't know how to handle his son or what will happen to him during a transition. John's afraid the new plant manager will quit because of Adam before he transitions from the business. Janice tells him that she needs to have some security about her future at Aardvark. She worried about having the company sold and that she'll be fired. He owes her peace of mind at least.

These issues are staring him in the face, the biggest of which, he has a nagging feeling he doesn't have enough cash to retire. He knows it, and he's afraid to let anyone else in on his dark secret. His wife thinks they have plenty of money because of the growth and profits and that John can retire whenever he wants. But that's so not the case, not if John knows better.

John wants to transfer the company to his family. He can't figure out how his son fits in with this, nor does he have any idea about how they would pay him for it. He can't afford to just give them the business, and he doesn't want to anyway.

He knows his managers also have concerns. Janice has come right out and told him that she does, and John strongly suspects everyone else is concerned that if the business is sold, they will lose their jobs.

That's what really has him today. How will he ever manage to retire, and will his non-financial goals ever be filled? There has to be a key to both mysteries if he ever wants to ride off into the sunset.

John knows he needs help, and he knows whom to call. He hasn't talked with Aaron for over a year. Life keeps getting in the way, and he just never seems to get around to it. He'd enjoyed working with him six years ago, even though Aaron tends to be a bit too direct for John's taste. At least he isn't ever at a loss for knowing where Aaron's coming from! Both Alicia and Janice appreciate Aaron's broad business knowledge. Why not keep them happy as well? Maybe it is time to call him in for a day.

But first, he has to find Aaron's number.

John opens his desk and rummages around in the drawer where he keeps his business cards. He can never find a business card when he needs them.

More than a few horrified bystanders have told him he should put these cards into a database so he can easily find them, but John waves them off, partially out of plain old stubbornness, partially because he just enjoys the break in his workday that looking for the business cards gives him. He sputters at himself for being such a dope. How can he have lost Aaron's card in this mess?

John stopped looking and calls his attorney for the number. That's who'd introduced him to Aaron in the first place.

John says to his attorney, "I need to get Aaron's number from you. I've managed to misplace his card and think it's time for him to come in for a tune-up."

John gets the number from his attorney and, with encouragement from him, plans to call Aaron today.

Just as John picks up the phone again to call Aaron, in walks his wife, Ann. She doesn't so much walk into the office as breezes in. There's an airy feeling about her unless she's mad, then she resembles a hurricane.

She sits down in one of John's overstuffed chairs. "I just stopped by to say hi. What're you up to?"

John holds up a number scrawled on scrap paper. "I'm about to call Aaron and see if he has time for us again. The consultant."

Ann furrows her brow. John knows she has mixed feelings about Aaron.

"It's nice that your friend Aaron helped you make the company more successful. I will not, however, allow him to get you to fire Adam. And I know he was pushing you in that direction before. It's just not going to happen, so don't even think about it." Ann folds her arms across her chest. "What do you need to bring him back for? I thought everything was going so well here."

Before he could answer, Adam comes flying into the room in his usual torn t-shirt. He ignores his mother. "Either he goes or I go," he shouts at John.

John knows exactly who "he" is. He is the new plant manager, George Johnson.

John knows exactly what the issue is. George wants Adam to put together written procedures for maintenance on the older machinery in the plant. Adam refuses. John bets George has once again told Adam he needs the documentation.

From where John sits, he thinks George is more in the right than Adam. They need documentation, especially on the older machines. Adam is the only one who has the knowledge to fix those machines, and if Adam is out for any reason, the plant stops if one of them goes down.

John glares at his son. "Are you ever going to learn to knock?" He uses his are-you-kidding-me tone. "Can't you see your mother and I are having a conversation?" He stretches his hand toward Ann. "I'll deal with you and your latest George issue after. Now leave us alone."

With that, Adam storms out of the office, slamming the door behind him. John can hear him grumbling all the way down the hall.

Ann is no longer giving off a breezy vibe. John decides it's time to drive the point home anyway. "You just saw one reason I think we need to bring Aaron back. I'm not willing to lose our plant manager. If Adam keeps carrying on the way he is, that's precisely what's going to happen."

Ann purses her lips and folds her arms across her chest once again. "I don't understand why you constantly choose your non-family employees over our son. I'm sick of the way you treat him."

John opens his mouth to argue. He loves his wife, and their disagreements about their son is the one hot button that sends him into orbit.

"And I'm not willing to have that consultant come in here and tell you what to do with my son." And with this statement, Ann jerks herself from the chair and heads toward the door.

"Now wait one minute…" John says to the slamming door.

After what seems like an eternity, John picks up the phone.

Within a few rings, Aaron answers the phone. "Hi John, long time no talk. How're things going?" Aaron knows he'll likely hear that things aren't going especially well. That's how it usually is when a client calls him after a long hiatus.

"I need your help, or at least I think I do."

In short order, the two men have a plan in place to meet the following Tuesday.

CHAPTER 2

The Alignment Conversation

● ● ●

Tuesday rolls around before John knows it. He arrives at his office at 8:30, looks at some emails, and impatiently waits. He expects that Aaron will be right on time. Last time they worked together, Aaron would always say, "Late is five minutes early," and John assumes that mantra is true today.

Just as John is staring out the window looking at the parking lot, he sees Aaron get out of his car. Aaron drives a nice car, nothing fancy, and that is one thing John likes about Aaron. He doesn't need to show off how successful or smart he is.

Upon entering the building, Aaron notices the same receptionist from the last time he visited three years ago. He thinks to himself that John and his company must have made some giant strides in making their people feel valued. Last time around, every time he came to the office, there would be a different person at the receptionist's desk., "How are you doing today?" Aaron says to the receptionist. "Long time no see. I'm Aaron, and I'm here to see John." Aaron pauses for a second or two and then asks, "It seems like you've been at this job for a while. How have things changed in the last couple of years?"

The receptionist looks skeptical. She picks up the phone and tells John that Aaron is waiting for him.

Aaron smiles. "Don't mind me. I'm just being nosey."

She decides to answer Aaron's question. "Better than when I first started. I don't feel like I have to walk on eggshells and always watch what I say. Not anymore."

"I'm glad to hear that it's easier for you to do your job."

With that, John walks into the reception area and greets Aaron. "Aaron, how are you? It's been a long time. Has life been good for you?"

"Life's been good. From what your receptionist tells me, things are better for you. Why don't we go to your office and catch up?"

While they walk to John's office, Aaron notices that things have visibly changed. The building is much bigger, which he spotted from the road, and the place looks cleaner. It has an entirely different feel. Instead of people walking by and averting his gaze, they look at the two of them and say hello or good morning. This makes him believe that people are probably feeling less like they're always waiting for the other shoe to drop or for someone to either yell or criticize them.

The two men enter John's office. John closes the door, and Aaron takes in the room. He notices that John has redecorated his office and has new furniture. John set up the office more like a living room with a desk at the end where John works when he's by himself. Clearly, John has taken Aaron's advice about designing an office to change the nature of conversations with visitors.

Aaron sits down in an overstuffed chair as John sits on the couch next to him. John grins. "This was another one of your ideas, one I first thought was crazy." He points at the arrangement as if he can read Aaron's mind. "I've almost stopped having meetings in our conference room unless it's a big meeting. In fact, two of our conference rooms now look more like living rooms than conference rooms."

Aaron starts. "John, I have to assume that you didn't ask me to spend the day with you to discuss all the great things that have happened at Aardvark since my last visit. What's up, and how can I help you?"

John fidgets in his chair. He hates to be vulnerable, and he knows that with Aaron he will be vulnerable or Aaron will force it out of him. John needs to be honest. "Well, from the outside, things seem to be going well. From the inside of my head, we're not even close to doing things well. I've only filled two of the four buckets of profit I committed to filling last time you and I worked together. I have a great lifestyle, which is bucket one. We've put together an emergency fund that will last us for six months, so bucket two is in good shape. I've got a growth program that's funded at about 60% and luckily the bank has stepped in and funded the rest of what we need, which means we're almost there with bucket three. The thing that keeps me up at night is that I've not done much to make sure I can be financially free from my business. Bucket four has not been getting enough attention, or it sure feels that way to me. I'm afraid that if I don't pay attention to bucket three and four, there is no way I'll ever be able to leave the business.

"In addition, my son is still at it, but there's a new twist in that saga. Janice recruited a new plant manager about six months ago. He's unbelievable. He's a trained SCRUM master and has a great understanding of the other process improvement programs out there. He's done a great job eliminating waste from our operations, which is the whole purpose of SCRUM."

John goes on to explain the problematic nature of George and Adam's relationship, the problem it's creating at the plant and at home with Ann. The ultimatum she's made that if one of them has to go, it won't be Adam, but George.

Right on cue, the door slams open and Adam storms into the room and screams at his father. "Dad, if you don't get that horrible person out of here, I'll quit. I'm sick and tired of dealing with idiots."

John's face turns red. "Did you see that my door was closed? Do you think it was closed so you could just barge in? And do you see that we have a guest here? I'll deal with this later. I'm in the middle of a meeting and don't have time for your behavior. Besides, how many times have I told you? If you have a problem with George, talk to Janice. I'm out of the loop on this. This is between you two."

With that, Adam turns on his heels and slams the door behind him, a repeat performance he appears to be making for Aaron.

Aaron takes off his glasses and cleans them while thinking about what to say. "Well, I see some things haven't changed around here. I'd guess that one thing you'd like to see change is Adam's behavior here."

John sighs and nods his head.

"Is there anything else we need to discuss today?"

John says, "Ann wants me to retire and turn the business over to the kids. I think Alicia could run the business, but I'm scared that if both Adam and Alicia are in business together, our family will blow apart and the company will disappear."

He lists the other issues—the blame game everyone plays, including him; the excess of cash to support their current growth but no more; the good profits but poor cash flow. "I'm not sure how I'll ever save enough to retire, and I'm not sure that if I sell the business to the kids, there'll be enough cash to pay me out so I can afford to retire."

When John stops speaking, Aaron lets silence take over for about thirty seconds. "It looks like we've just gone over in one hour what it took us an entire day the first time we met. I don't know if you realized it, but you just gave me a good description of where you are now and what your issues are. Since we're already in the alignment conversation, why don't we go to stage 2?"

Aaron's reference to the alignment conversation confused John. "I should know what an alignment conversation is, but for the life of me, I can't remember what it is."

Aaron realizes he just broke one of his cardinal rules. Whenever he uses a process he's named or used jargon, he needs to assume the person he's speaking with doesn't know the meaning. "I apologize. I got ahead of myself and forgot that six years is a long time to remember all of my processes.

"The alignment conversation has four main parts. First, where are you now? That's what we just went over. Second, where do you want to be? We ask this using the famous Strategic Coach question: If we were to get together three years from now, what would have to happen for you to be personally and economically successful? That's what we're about to do. We then move to the third, looking at the difference between where you are now and where you want to be. Finally, we figure out what the value to you is if you bridge that gap. Does that make sense?"

"I remember. Yes, let's keep going."

"It's now time for you to do some forward thinking. If we could handle the issues we've talked about so far, what would the future look like for you?"

"Well, I'd know I had enough predictable cash so I could leave the business if I wanted. I would have a strategy in place for transferring the business. I would know how the senior managers would all work together after I'm gone. Ann and I would have figured out how to live together with me no longer coming to work every day. We'd be on the same page when it comes to Adam. And I'd know what I needed to do to transfer the business and keep my family together." John feels the weight lift from his shoulders just envisioning this outcome.

"Those are all great things," Aaron says, making some notes. "So, if you were to have all of those issues solved in a way that keeps everyone happy, what would it be worth to you? I'm asking this, knowing that it will be hard for you to put a dollar value on what it's worth. So, instead of a dollar value, what would be the psychic value to have all of those issues solved?"

John has never specifically thought about the psychic value of solving issues. He isn't even sure what a psychic value is. "Another dumb question. What do you mean by a psychic value?"

Aaron once again reminds himself that what he thinks everyone knows isn't necessarily so. "Psychic value is the emotional value; how you would feel and what you'd be doing differently if all of the things we talked about came true."

John has to stop and think for a while. "If we could accomplish all of the things we're talking about, I'd have less pressure. My relationship with Ann would be better. I'd have a great relationship with Alicia and a better one with Adam. My kids would get along well with each other.

And Adam would be happy. He just isn't happy and hasn't been for years." The force of the statement about Adam takes John by surprise. He hasn't realized how important his son's well-being is to him.

"I'd also have confidence that the company would last for another generation, that it would produce enough cash to allow me to become financially free from my business. Our company would continue to grow, stay profitable, and create a lot more cash. I think that's a pretty good list for now."

Aaron agrees. "I think you've done a great job. We're clear on the psychic value. Now, we get to the hard part. One, do you want some help with these issues?"

Hesitating, John nods. He finds the question odd.

"Next, would you like me to help you with the stuff we've talked about today?"

John looks at Aaron like he's crazy. "That is why I asked you to come in. I know what you charge, and I know what you can do. I don't expect miracles, and I think you can truly help us."

Aaron smiles, and although the questions about whether John wants to work with him might be obvious, it's always best to have the client tell Aaron what he wants. It's the whole reason he always asks, no matter how often he's worked with people, whether they want help and if they want Aaron to help him. He's even had some people say yes and no to those questions. Aaron knows it's just always better to check in on things like that.

"Great. Then here's what I'd like to have the rest of the day look like. I'd like to have a conversation with Janice, your new plant manager, and Alicia about what they'd like to see happen. And I'd like to spend an hour with Ann.

"The mistake we made last time was not bringing Ann into the conversation. She may not work here, but her influence is here in a big way. We want to acknowledge this. And let her know that we value what she thinks, that we need her help, that we want her to be happy with what's going on. Without her involvement, any plan we put together will fail."

John thinks all the requests Aaron made are reasonable and agrees to them.

CHAPTER 3

Aaron Meets with the Managers and Alicia

● ● ●

As they walk down the hall to the conference room, Aaron notices the pictures of Aardvark employees and the date they started their job, along with the number of years they've worked at the company. From a quick calculation, Aaron can see that Aardvark's turnover rate has gone way down. That's always a good sign. In front of the conference room, Aaron spies a board listing each company value with a clarifying statement about what each value means.

Before going into the conference room, Aaron asks John how often he refers to the values on the wall. John stops, strokes his chin, and says, "At least three or four times a week. That's when things are going well. When I have a problem, I refer to them way more often. I've found them to be a really helpful tool. In fact, this might be the most useful long-term thing we did last time we worked together."

With that, John leaves Aaron to meet with the managers, having talked through the pros and cons of having him in the meeting. They'd come to the conclusion that his presence would keep the managers and Alicia from telling Aaron what they really think. Of course, John thinks his people tell him what they think all the time. Aaron knows they don't. This time, Aaron wins out.

Aaron enters the room with a huge grin on his face. He has business to attend to. Both Janice and Alicia greet him warmly. Aaron sees a new person in the room he hasn't met. He figures it must be George Johnson, the new plant manager. Aaron bounds over to where the man is standing, and with a broad smile and sticks out his hand. "Hi George, I'm Aaron. So glad you could take some time to meet with us this morning. I'm looking forward to hearing what you have to say about your experience at Aardvark over the past eighteen months."

George shrugs and takes a seat. Apparently, George isn't wild about joining this meeting. When Aaron asks, George explains that he has some major problems in the plant and thinks his time could be better spent with his people.

From George's response, Aaron comes to the conclusion that George thinks he's going to be called on the carpet for the poor relationship he has with John's son, Adam.

Aaron motions for everyone to take a seat at the table. The table is new, built of solid mahogany. It has all the high-tech bells and whistles that expensive conference tables have. He thinks it's nice that John has loosened the purse strings to spruce up the facility. He also wonders whether some of John's lack of retirement funds are due to him having loosened up a little too much.

After everyone settles in, Aaron starts. "It's good to see everyone. George, you may have heard about the work we did here several years ago. I'm hoping what you heard wasn't all bad."

Janice pipes up. "Things are better around here. Sales are good, profits are up, and all of us enjoy our work, or at least I do."

Aaron smiles. "Great, I'm glad to hear that. Now, today I'd like to repeat what we did when I first came here six years ago. I'd like to take another crack at having an alignment conversation with you." Aaron reminds the group what they'll be covering. "From what I gather, there's a lot more trust between all of you compared to the last time. That should make life a lot easier."

Both Janice and Alicia nod. George looks a little confused.

Janice jumps in. "George, the last time Aaron was here things were really a mess. I had your job and was thinking of quitting. Alicia had just joined the company, and she hadn't gotten her formal schooling beaten out of her yet, so many of her ideas just weren't very practical. John was the bottleneck in everything. All decisions had to flow through him and, most of the time, the decisions John made were from the seat of his pants and not thought out very well."

George takes the information in. "Glad I wasn't here back then. I'm having enough problems as it is. It's tough when things seem to change almost every day."

Aaron gets where George is coming from. "That's privately held companies. They're all like that. The good news is they're very flexible in how they go about doing things. The bad news is they're very flexible, and rules seem to change a lot or get ignored altogether."

George nods in agreement.

Aaron continues. "Let's get down to work." Aaron looks at Janice. "Why don't you start us off?"

Janice appears ready. Clearly, John prepared her for the meeting with Aaron. "Thankfully, things are running pretty smoothly right now. John has become a good delegator. He mostly stays out of the way and lets us do what's right for the company. Every once in a while, he goes back to his old ways. But he's been great about letting me point that out to him when it happens.

"Alicia is doing a great job with marketing, and the marketplace is really seeing us as the leaders we've always been." She turns and acknowledges George. "Adding George has made my life infinitely easier." She thinks for another moment. "Oh, and I've even learned enough about finance to be dangerous."

Everyone at the table laughs. George gives her a thumbs up.

"We still have one major personnel problem, which I'm hoping George will talk about." From what Aaron can see, Janice no longer looks nervous referencing Adam at these meetings. "And none of us really know what John's strategy is as he gets older. In fact, my biggest concern right now is how he plans to handle succession for the company. He keeps saying he wants to keep the business in the family, but as far as I can see, he's done nothing about it."

Aaron pours himself a glass of water and takes a sip. "I'm so glad to hear that John is now a reasonably good delegator. And, I'm glad you see that the biggest rock to push up the hill is the succession work. That's why John brought me in."

Aaron moves his gaze to Alicia. She appears to be prepared as well. No doubt she thinks she is the natural one to take over the business.

"I also think things are going well here." Alicia says, sitting up in her seat. "I've learned so much about marketing. None of it came from what I learned in my MBA program. We just don't have the budget to do what they taught me in school. I've learned how to get the most from just a few dollars we can afford to spend." She slows down and seems to consider her choice of words. "I'm also wondering when my father will get around to giving up control of the company." She turns toward Janice. Aaron can see how much Alicia respects her mentor. "I'd love to see him promote Janice. She should be President of the company. That way he can take more of a back seat." She bites her lip. "When I bring it up to him, he gets angry and accuses me of trying to force him out."

Finally, Aaron looks at George. "George, it's your turn."

George shifts in his chair. He looks at Alicia and Janice, and then at Aaron. Aaron guesses he's calculating how much he can share with a consultant he doesn't know and doesn't trust.

"There are days I love working here, and there are days I consider walking into Janice's office and quitting on the spot."

From the horrified look playing across Janice's face, this is clearly the first time she's heard this statement coming from George.

George continues. "I love what this company does. The quality of our products is first class. Most of the people here are first class people to work with. I've been having a good time instituting new programs that have made us much more effective. Janice has been hugely supportive." George abruptly stops talking and stares at Aaron.

"There seems to be something you wanted to say but haven't said yet. I can even guess what that something might be," Aaron says.

From the look on his face, George is going through mental calculations and some risk evaluation. "It's just that I have an impossible problem with Adam. At any other company I've ever worked at, someone like Adam would be escorted out the door and never let back in again. He's arrogant, and he has this wonderful ability to turn off anyone he comes into contact with. I'm sorry to have to say that." George appears genuinely sorry. "He may be brilliant at what he does, but if we can't help him become a useful member of the team, it's only a matter of time. Either he leaves or I'll leave." George stops speaking and looks like he just swallowed a frog.

Aaron nods in George's direction, letting him know he appreciates his comment. Then he looks at each member at the table. "Let's just say that's something we've already agreed we need to solve this time around. I don't know what that solution will be, and Adam's current behavior can't continue. That being said, let's move on to where we want to be in four and a half years."

"Four and a half years?" Janice laughs. "I'm always amused the way you use weird numbers when we're talking about something in the future." She turns toward Alicia. "You're the one who'll eventually be at the helm, so why don't you start and let us know what you're thinking."

Alicia straightens her posture. "I'd like to see myself on the way to becoming the CEO of the company. I need to gain some more experience in other areas of the business. I'd like to see a plan in place for us to transfer ownership of the company over to me."

Aaron says. "That sounds like a great plan. George, your thoughts?"

"I've never really thought about what I want to happen here in four years or four and a half years, let alone what I want to have happen here in one year. So, I'll just have to wing it, as if my opinion counts. Again, I'd like to see the problem with Adam solved. I'd also like to see us become at least 20% more effective in our plant. And I'd love to see the amount of work we have coming in doubled over that period. I've got some ideas I want to work on, but we just don't have the cash yet to do them." He folds his hands on the table when he's done.

Finally, Aaron looks at Janice. "It's your turn."

"Like Alicia, I'd like to see a real succession plan in place. I'd like to know what my future with the company would look like when or if Alicia becomes the CEO." Janice gives Alicia a guarded smile. "I'd like to know that when my time with Aardvark is over, I'll be financially independent. I'd love to have looked back at the last, ok, four and a half years and see that it was the most productive and interesting time I've spent in my career. I mean, if you're asking me what I want."

The managers go back and forth discussing additional concerns and observations. Aaron looks at all three and is once again impressed with how often people he works with share their real thoughts during this exercise. It's time for Aaron to wrap up this meeting. He's scheduled to meet with Ann in just a few minutes.

CHAPTER 4

Ann and Aaron Come to an Agreement

● ● ●

For some reason, John's office door is shut. When Aaron knocks, John shouts for him to come in. Entering, he spots Ann chatting with John.

"Ann, you remember Aaron don't you?"

Ann smirks. "How could I forget him? He tried to get you to fire our son."

Aaron raises an eyebrow. He thought he'd smoothed that out over lunch the last time he was there, but clearly he was wrong. "Perhaps we could start off on a better foot this time." He takes his usual seat. "You believe my goal is to get rid of your son. I can promise you, it's not. My only goal is to do what's best for both your son and the company." He then addresses John. "I'm really enthused about what I heard from the team. They're all very excited about what's going on around here. I think you've done some great work."

John ignores the comment. He moves from behind the desk. "Aaron, where would be a good place for you and Ann to spend some time together?"

Aaron says, "How about the conference room?"

With that, Aaron and Ann head to the conference room. Aaron lets Ann choose her seat. She sits right in the middle of the table. Instead of sitting across from her, Aaron chooses a seat next to her. Ann seems a little unnerved by his action. Aaron knows that by sitting next to her, he takes down a potential non-verbal barrier. The conversation is likely going to be a tough one, and he wants to take any steps he can to compensate.

"Ann, last time I saw you the company and John were in a very different place than today. I'm sorry I left you with the feeling that I was after your son. I can see how it would appear that way. The truth is, I wasn't. My only concern was to have your husband be in less pain and the company be more successful. This time around, I think my job will be very different."

Aaron then explains the alignment conversation and tells Ann that his purpose is to find out what her concerns and dreams are.

"John has brought me back to help him think through a succession process that works for everyone. Now, I've learned over the years that if I don't include the spouse and understand his or her needs and wants, the entire plan will blow up. I know you're not involved in the day-to-day operation of the business, but I know you and John talk about the business. Probably way more than you really want to. So, your input is important to the company, your husband, family, and even me."

Ann takes a deep breath. She seems to relax just a little. Her face softens. "To tell you the truth, I really didn't want to come in and talk with you today. My inputs won't matter. John will do what John will do. He always ends up doing what he wants to do, no matter what I say."

Leaning back in his chair, Aaron relaxes as well. "I can see how that might happen. I can also tell you that if he doesn't listen to you and take your feelings into account, any succession plan we come up with will be much tougher on John than it needs to be. I'll be working with him to help him understand how important you and your opinions are."

She seems to take that in.

"Ann, if I were to ask you where you are today with your relationship with John and the business, what would your answer be?"

Ann pauses, looks at the ceiling. After two or three beats, she finally turns and faces him. "Well, things are better than last time you were here. John and I have been taking regular vacations, and he's only working about forty-five hours a week. I keep wondering what he's doing working those hours. He seems to have things pretty well set around here and has done a good job of taking himself away from being in the middle of everything. And as far as our relationship goes, it's much better."

She runs her hand across the smooth mahogany surface of the table. "The business seems to be doing well, and I haven't heard John complain about not having enough money to run the business for at least three years. I'm not sure he's saving enough for us to retire, and that's been a bone of contention between us." She waves her hand toward the artwork on the walls. Aaron hadn't noticed them during the previous meeting. Apparently the framed paintings were expensive if Ann was pointing them out.

"But, when it comes to our son, nothing has changed. If possible, it's even gotten worse. He recently hired this guy George to run the plant. Adam keeps telling me how incompetent he is. How the fellow doesn't have a clue what needs to be done around here. When I bring this up to John, he just shuts me down and tells me I have no idea what I'm talking about. That I need to stop listening to Adam. He keeps telling me that Adam is the problem, and if he were anyone else, he would have fired him long ago." Her voice gets louder each time she says Adam's name.

Aaron lets a little silence fill the room before responding. "Do you think Adam is happy?"

The question seems to take Ann aback. Her immediate reaction is to insist that Adam is happy. Many seconds goes by. She tells Aaron that she needs to think for a minute or two. She studies the pictures before turning back to Aaron. "You know, I've never thought about that. He might not be. I often wonder if he has an inferiority complex. You know, he never went to college. His sister has an MBA and seems to do nothing wrong in their father's eye. I bet that really gets under Adam's skin. We've never really talked about it, Adam and I, except when he's having one of his temper tantrums. Then he blames his father for everything and screams, claims that John always treats his sister better than he's been treated. That's hard for me to argue with. I guess he probably isn't always very happy." Aaron can tell it makes her sad to say this. He thinks the anger is just a cover for Ann's sadness.

"When Adam was in school, he never did very well. He was always that kid who was getting into trouble. I just couldn't get him to study. At the same time, he was great with his hands. He'd come into the shop with John and, from a very young age, he could fix almost anything. John hasn't given him enough credit. He's great at pointing out his weak points, though. That's for sure." She pulls a clean glass from the tray and pours herself a glass of water.

Aaron thinks about what he's just heard. "I hear a lot of pain in your voice." Ann waves his statement away. Furrows her brow. "I think Adam is in a lot of pain."

Ann stiffens. No doubt she wasn't expecting any sort of sympathy from anyone, least of all Aaron.

After a pause, Aaron says, "So, let's go forward three years. If we were to get together three years from now, how would life be, and how would it differ from today? In a perfect world."

Ann takes a deep breath, "First, of course, I want Adam to be happy. That's the biggest issue right now. Second,

I want John to figure out what his next act in life will be. I can't have him just hanging around the house after he retires. Frankly, I'm not sure he even has much of an interest in retiring anyway, so maybe my worry is silly. He really doesn't have that many hobbies. No way he can fill all of his time playing golf and riding his bike, I don't care what he says."

"What about you?" Aaron smiles. "What do you want for yourself three years from now?"

Ann once again slips into silence while she thinks. It impresses Aaron how thoughtful Ann is during the conversation. He loves it when people think before they speak.

"For me, well, let me see. I'd like to spend more time traveling. I'd like John to listen to me more." She laughs here. "I'd like Adam to not yell at me about these problems. And I'd like Alicia to make sure that what she's doing is what she really wants to do. She spends way too much time trying to please her father."

Ann pauses, "The truth is, I'm quite happy with my life. There's not much I want to do that I put on hold or don't do." She seems to reconsider Aaron. She leans an elbow on the armrest between them. "That's one reason I'm worried about John retiring. I've put together a life where he's not there most of the time. I love John and love the time we spend together. Our time together is not hours and hours, it's more minutes and minutes. Spending more time together will be a big change for both of us. I guess I'd like to see us figure out how that would work."

Ann has given Aaron, knowingly or unknowingly, a great road map for how to work with John and even how to help Adam. He's pretty sure Alicia is on the right path for her, so he considers that concern a non-issue. At the same time Aaron knows that Alicia has a long way to go and there's potential roadblocks along the way. He's got a good sense for what the engagement will look like and is ready to talk to John about next steps.

He turns to Ann. "It's a huge honor to talk with you. Thank you."

With that, Aaron walks Ann out to her car and lets her know how much he's looking forward to their next meeting.

CHAPTER 5

Creating the Master Project List

● ● ●

The next day, the two men sit in John's office drinking coffee. Aaron thinks it's best to recap the previous day's conversations and to set the tone for today's work, which is introducing John to the eight steps he'll have to go through to make sure any succession plan he puts together will be successful. John knows this is important. He's seen too many of his friends have businesses that were going to transfer and, at the last minute, everything fell apart.

Settling into their respective chairs in the comfortable part of the office, John waits for Aaron to start the conversation.

Aaron begins. "Why don't we start with what I discovered during my alignment conversations yesterday? First, let me start with the one you and I had.

"There are four things you want to make sure we accomplish. You want to make sure we have enough cash created by the company to fill the four buckets of profit. You want a solution for handling your son and keeping Ann on your side. You want to figure out who should and will be the successor owner of your business. The final thing you want is to figure out how you and Ann will live with each other since you won't be at work as much.

"Two of these areas Ann and I also talked about."

John asked, "Which ones?" He was genuinely curious.

"She wants to know how you and Adam can coexist. And she wants to know how you two will get along, what with all the free time you'll have once you retire. She's concerned about her life changing as a result of you not working full-time, or even part-time."

John has to let that sink in. He hasn't really thought about Ann when he considers his exit from the business. He's just assumed she'll want him around more. The news that she might not is something he'll need to get his head around. What does that actually mean? John raises an eyebrow. He shouldn't be surprised that Ann is concerned about the two of them getting in each other's way after he steps away, but he is.

"Now, let's move on to what the managers thought was important. I bet you won't find many of the things on the managers' list that will surprise you."

Aaron works with enough owners to know who has a finger on the pulse of the managers and who doesn't. John often acts like he isn't paying attention or doesn't have a clue, but he knows which way the wind blows and is well aware of what his managers are thinking about most of the time.

"Oh, and at some point we'll have to bring this conversation in to cover all of your managers. The three I talked with yesterday are concerned about five things. Now, this will come as no surprise: Adam was brought up by everyone as a problem."

John throws up a hand. He gets it, but it's not like he knows what to do about it.

"I might have some ideas about what we can do with Adam. I want to make sure I talk with him first, however." Aaron then fills John in on the other wants and needs of the managers. "Alicia and Janice are wondering about what you're going to do for a succession plan. They want the specifics for how you'll release control. Mind you, I didn't get the sense that they want to force you out. Regardless, Alicia in particular wants to know what the next step is for her to become CEO. She definitely wants to make Aardvark her long-term focus. But she doesn't see a clear path. I have an idea about her next step, and I'll want to talk about that later."

John wants to jump in here but bites his tongue. He makes a mental note to come back to this subject. He knows it's time for Alicia to take her next step; he just isn't sure what that step should be. He's curious what Aaron's idea is.

Aaron continues. "Janice is wondering whether you plan to replace her with Alicia. I told her she's not likely going to lose her role as Chief Operating Officer in the near or even distant future."

"Finally, everyone, and especially Alicia, wants to know who is going to be the future owner or owners of the company. Alicia is hesitant about being co-owner with her brother. She's worried about the potential fireworks. She's been on the receiving end of too many of his tantrums. If that's what's in store for her, she may not go forward."

John listens carefully. He wants to jump right in and start solving the problems. Just before he opens his mouth, he remembers Aaron's other meeting, the one he had with Ann. "What did Ann have to say yesterday? She came home all excited about her conversation with you."

Aaron has to think about how much to share with John. He likes to make sure conversations he has with others in a business remain confidential. He wants to ask Ann for permission to share what they talked about before he tells John the details of the conversation. He knows he can share the conversation in general terms and can get permission for details later. He also knows that he needs to have John understand how important it is for Ann to be on board. If she's not, the plan will fall apart. He's seen that happen too often early in his career and knows that if she's not on board, nothing will work.

John says, "She wouldn't tell me what you talked about. But it would seem that she no longer wants your head served up on a silver platter. What happened?"

Aaron finds it interesting that Ann didn't want to tell John about their conversation. His guess is Ann didn't want to get into it about Adam. It would appear that any time there's an incident that involves Adam, particularly if it involved other members of the family, it always blows up.

Aaron answers. "I thought the conversation with Ann was very useful. I set out with the intention of resetting our relationship. There's no surprise in her list of concerns. In fact, they're very similar to what you and the managers want. And, of course, the Adam issue came up. His unhappiness."

Before John has a chance to respond, Aaron continues with his recap. "I know we talked about this before, and I want to bring it up again. Ann has a life for herself. I'm not convinced and would be willing to bet some real money that she's not interested in having her life disrupted by you retiring.

"You've worked at least sixty hours a week ever since you started this company. Now that you're down to about forty-five hours, you're still gone more than you're home. She's built a life outside of you, and she's worried that you're going to disrupt her life. I wouldn't worry about her not loving you. It's something you're going to have to work on, and it might be the hardest part of the transition work we do together."

It's John's turn to sit in silence for a while. He could have figured out most of what Aaron has told him if he took the time to think about it. He realizes that he hasn't been all that curious about what others think, particularly Ann, because he's always felt he's had bigger problems to solve. But really, many of Ann's concerns are the same as his. They might argue more than he likes, but Ann has a good head on her shoulders.

Aaron interrupts John's thoughts. "Why don't we put together a list of everybody's concerns and see how that fits into the things that we might want to work on?" Aaron then pulls out a notepad.

The two men talk through a master list of possible projects.

1. Making sure Aardvark has enough excess cash to provide for all the needs John and the business have.

2. Coming up with a solution that will make all interested parties happy with Adam.

3. Coming up with a strategy that will allow Adam to be happy with his life.

4. Figuring out who will be the successor owner of the company.

5. Figuring out how Ann and John can live together with John being around more than ever before.

6. Having clarity about Alicia's path at the company. Will she become CEO and if so, how will that happen?

7. Having a plan for Janice so she can retire from Aardvark financially independent. Figuring out her role as Alicia takes over control of the company.
8. Putting together a financial plan that shows how much money needs to be saved and where income will come from after transitioning ownership of the company.
9. Helping Ann understand that George likely is not the problem when it comes to Adam.

As they put together the list, John realizes that there are an awful lot of things that need attention. "How in the world are we ever going to accomplish them all? In fact, some of them seem to be impossible problems to solve. Take Adam, for example. We all know he's a problem; we just have no idea how to solve it."

Aaron has some ideas about the Adam issue. "Let's not get sidetracked on that just yet. As we go through a process I want to explain to you, we'll be sure to come back to Adam. I'm hopeful that my ideas will bear fruit.

CHAPTER 6

Cash Flow Concerns

● ● ●

On the way to the break room, Aaron notices that there's much less material just hanging around the plant waiting to be used. He also notices that everyone in the plant is wearing a uniform. The uniforms are sharp and clean, like the surroundings.

Aaron's curious. "Last time I was here, everything was out of place and your employees were wearing anything they wanted. I'm impressed with the change. When you've got visitors and customers on site, I'm betting they're really impressed with the way your facility looks."

John stops to look around. "Yes, and I have to give credit to Janice for the change. She was the one who pitched me on the idea shortly after we last worked together. We didn't go all in at first, but over the past several years we've kept trying small changes that improve the way the place looks. I have to say, it's been a raging success. It's funny how those small experiments add up to big results."

Aaron strokes his chin. "I noticed something yesterday. Is there a reason everyone's in uniform except Adam?"

"Not really, except that he refuses to wear a uniform. He thinks being a slob is a way for him to bond with the folks who work in the plant. The truth is he's seen as a jerk for bucking the rules, and I can't seem to get that information into his thick skull." John shakes his head in frustration.

The two men round the corner and enter the break room. This part of the plant had been completely redone. With pride radiating off of him, John points out some of the biggest changes.

"Most of what you see is Ann's handiwork. She likes to tell everyone she has nothing to do with the company. That's not completely true. She's the one in charge of remodeling for the most part, even though she thinks we're spending money we shouldn't be on these projects." John knows his defensiveness is showing. "I have to say the changes have also paid off in our productivity. If you amortize the costs for these changes, they more than make up for the money we've spent." He flicks on the coffee machine button and grabs a couple of paper cups. "Let's take a seat away from everyone and talk here for a few minutes." He waves at a group of employees seated at a table enjoying a snack. They all wave back.

John and Aaron grab their coffee. "Before I get into the eight steps to create a sale ready company, there are a few other things I would like to talk about," Aaron says, looking for the creamer.

"A sale ready company?"

Aaron digs a spoon into a large Cremora jar. "A sale ready company is one that someone else would want to own but is not necessarily for sale. It's where we get your company ready to be sold to an outside party, even though we have no intention of doing so. It's really just an extension of the sustainable business work we did last time I was here."

John thinks he could find a buyer for his business tomorrow, though his goal has always been to transfer it to the kids. But he knows from experience that Aaron may just prove him wrong, so he bites his tongue.

Aaron says, "The first thing we need to focus on is having excess cash flow. Not just enough cash to fill the daily needs of the owner and the business, but enough excess cash flow that excites a potential buyer. That gets a buyer thinking your company could be a cash machine."

"If it were a cash machine, we wouldn't be having this conversation," John says with a snort.

Aaron agrees. "Right now, it looks like you have enough cash for some things, like a remodel, but you're still robbing Peter to pay Paul. And, since you've already told me your preference is to sell the business to your children, you're going to have to depend on the next generation to create enough cash to not only run the business but also provide cash for your retirement. This means your business is going to have to create a lot more cash than it is right now."

John frowns. "If it were that easy."

"Let me ask you something. Are you monitoring your cash flow with the models we worked on last time I was here?" Aaron expects no answer, which he gets. "And, do you have a dashboard where you're watching the amount of free cash that you have grow on a weekly basis?"

John can't think of a time when Aaron didn't attach a question to his comments. Although he hasn't always liked Aaron's questions, he knows they help him get to the root of the issue quickly. He thinks for a minute. Why did he stop doing that stuff? "Well, we started down that road, but I just saw our checking account grow and figured that was a good enough thing to monitor. For the past three years or so, things have been good and I've not really had to worry about cash." He really had felt secure. Now, not nearly so much.

Aaron recalls his conversation with Ann. "Ann mentioned that she hadn't heard you complain about cash in over three years. That fits with what you just said. I'm going to bet that when we get together with your controller, we're going to hear a story that's a little different. So, I'll take the answer as no, you really aren't monitoring your cash flow statement, nor have you put together a cash monitoring dashboard either."

John shrugs.

"That's something we'll have to work on. We'll add that to the list of what we'll need to attend to if we're to have a sale ready company." Aaron pulls out a chair for John and one for himself. They both sit. "Here are the things we need to bring up to speed. And by that, I mean, we need to make sure they all score an 8 out of 10.

"Let's start with the easy stuff. We're going to need to figure out what the company is worth. That's easy because we take your free cash flow and come up with a multiple to use. Also, because we're planning on an internal sale, we'll eventually need to get a formal valuation done. We likely won't use this for the business value, but we'll need it for the IRS to make sure you're not selling your business for a bargain to your kids.

"We're also going to need to know who's going to buy it. Will it be just Alicia, or Alicia and Adam?"

John feels his stomach lurch. He's known that the decision would have to be made, and now that time has come. He knows his preference, but he doesn't want to deal with the blowback.

"We also need to make sure your key people stick around," Aaron continues. "We have some great tools for this. I'll get into this later with you and your team."

Aaron finishes with the three easy items on his list. Now, it's time to move to the things he considers more difficult, though easily done. "We need to make sure you stop raiding the emergency fund for capital improvements. I would rather see you borrow the money from the bank. I'm going to assume, based on your financials, this won't be much of an issue."

John is and has always been debt adverse. He hates borrowing money and only does it for business growth. Even then, he only borrows kicking and screaming about a downturn in business that could ruin them.

Aaron continues, "Getting you to do a financial plan has been on our list since last time I was here. It's not hard to do, but there seems to be something getting in the way."

John pauses. "It's just one of those things I never get around to. I see why it's important now, and I'll get it done. I have a suspicion Ann is also going to push me on this."

Aaron says, "Just make sure you take into account what you need to live on and have safety funds as well and funds earmarked for fun. When you first retire, you'll likely spend more money on going places you've wanted to go but have never made the time to go.

"Ann has a list a mile long. I've heard her mention Italy a dozen times this year alone." Italy is on John's list as well, and he's starting to look forward to more travel when he stops working.

"As you do your retirement financial plan, you'll need to start thinking like an investor rather than a business owner. You're going to need to have your financial advisor work with you to design an investment strategy that will allow you to create the cash you need to live on from the investments you have."

Aaron takes a deep breath. He's covered the doable stuff; now he needs to address the more difficult tasks.

"We have a few more things we need to cover. We suspect the business isn't creating enough excess cash, agreed?"

John reluctantly nods. He can hear the shift in tone and that makes him nervous.

"I'm going to recommend we go back and look at your profit and revenue drivers and see what needs to be fixed.

"We're also going to need to have a way to protect you and Ann when it comes time to sell the business. I don't want to get into the details just yet. It gets pretty technical. The simple version is this: Since you'll be the bank, you're going to have to act like a bank. In other words, there has to be an early warning system for you in place and ways for you to protect your investment until you're fully paid off."

John looks off and Aaron pauses. John isn't really sure what Aaron means by protecting his investment. He thinks that once the business is transferred, all of his money problems are over. He wants to drill down on this, but Aaron waves him off.

Aaron says, "The final thing is also the most difficult one. The final thing being what's next in your life. Ann is concerned about that, and you've let me know that you are too. This is the hardest part of any succession or transition plan. Everyone goes through what's known as seller's remorse. The difference is, for some, it's a real challenge that takes years to overcome. I'm hoping we can get you through this rough transition phase much more quickly."

John takes a sip of his coffee. He feels a little depressed. As Aaron finishes the list, a question pops into his mind.

How will he and the company ever be able to do all of the things Aaron listed?

Aaron spots the look on John's face and laughs. "I know it might feel impossible. In fact, I know that it does. But do you remember when I helped you come up with your to-do list the last time we worked together?"

John sighs.

Aaron looks at his watch. "Why don't we head back to your office and tackle each of the steps, match them to your needs? Wait. I've got one more to add to the list. Getting our arms around free cash at Aardvark."

It's now 10 a.m. John doesn't see how they'll get through all of these things in two hours. He has things to do this afternoon and is hoping Aaron can spend some time with his son. That's really the biggest problem he sees at Aardvark right now.

CHAPTER 7

John Learns If He Can Afford to Retire

● ● ●

John and Aaron step through the door into John's office. Why, Aaron wonders, does John keep it so dark? The frequency of John's sour moods would lessen if his office were brighter. Before he brings up the topic, he realizes that he needs to get through the eight steps of leaving your business. He doesn't have any time to waste, especially if he wants to also address the ten things they need to accomplish.

The two men take their usual seats. Aaron waits for a second before launching in. "John, let's go through each of the eight steps and see how each might be applied to your circumstances."

Aaron goes to the whiteboard. On the board he writes *Step #1: What Do You Need?*

"The first step is all about assessing what you need. Now, I'm not talking about what you need to feel happy, the emotional stuff, but what you need for assets that will allow you to leave your business, the financial stuff. In other words, what sort of cash flow will you need when you walk away, and where will that cash come from?"

Throwing up his hands, John laughs. "You cut straight to the chase, don't you?"

"This question came up several times when I was talking with both you and Ann. Straight to the chase or not, do you have a financial planner who can help you with this?"

John thinks about the guy he used for managing the 401(k) and some of his personal investments. "I do. A guy I've used over the years to manage our stuff. He's offered to do a financial plan for us for years. I've always put him off. It might be time for me to take him up on his offer."

Aaron always tries to work with his clients' advisors, as long as they're competent. The jury is out on John's fellow. "After you're done and you've left the business, you're going to want someone you can trust, someone who has your best interests at heart. This person needs to not only understand you but in the planning process has to know how to plan for a business owner like you."

Aaron continues. "Having what you need in place, which is the first stage of transitioning your business, is all about being financially free. There's a tool I developed years ago that can quickly help you find out whether you're on the path to being financially free from your company or not. It's called the four boxes of financial independence. We can sketch this out and get an answer to this question in the next ten minutes."

Aaron takes out a legal pad and draws four boxes on the top page. Then he fills in the numbers he's gathered from John's financials.

—The Business— $2,000,000 $1,500,000 after taxes @ 4% = $60,000	—Real Estate— $3,000,000 value Rent: $150,000 per year
—401(k) Plan— $500,000 @ 4% = $20,000	—Other Investments— $500,000 @ 4% = $20,000

"John, if I remember correctly when we did this exercise the last time I was here, these numbers didn't look nearly as promising. Last time, you said you needed about $200,000 per year to live on. Is that still the same number? Because these values here more than add up to that."

John doesn't want to tell Aaron but with the extra profits the company has brought in, he and Ann have improved their lifestyle. He frowns and looks at his shoes. "Well, we've sort of increased our standard of living. My guess is we now live on about $300,000 per year." He cracks a knuckle.

Aaron pauses. He hoped that John had maintained his original living standard. At the same time, it isn't hard to understand why they raised it. The company is highly profitable; though it might not be using its cash in the most effective way. John is like many of his other clients whose businesses had finally taken off.

"OK, let's see how our four-box analysis came out."

Aaron gets out of his chair and walks over to the whiteboard. He thinks it'll be easier and quicker if he just lists how John's income plays out in a linear format.

"Let's go through each of the components of the four boxes. First, we have your business. I'm going to assume that you'll save all of the money you get from the note your kids will have with you. You'll eventually end up with about $1,500,000 in today's value after you pay taxes. That's a pretty good estimate. If we use a financial planner's rule of thumb of spending 4% of that value per year, that'll give you $60,000 per year to spend." Aaron writes $60,000 on the whiteboard.

John understands completely.

"Next, let's look at the real estate you own. When you retire, there's no reason for you to sell your building. The building will be paid off in two years, which means you can use all of the cash flow from rent for your lifestyle. By my calculations, you should be getting $150,000 per year in rent. Since you'll have no debt and the company pays all of the building expenses including taxes, you get to keep all of it for retirement." Aaron then adds $150,000 to the list on the whiteboard, bringing the total to $210,000.

He knows what the property is worth, the rent the company would have to pay to occupy it if he didn't own it. Once again, John agrees with Aaron's assessment.

"Let's combine both your retirement plan and outside investments next. You'll have about $500,000 in both your investment account and 401(k). Using the 4% rule again, you'll be able to spend about $40,000 per year."

Aaron then adds up what John could spend and leaves out the sale of the business. That money wouldn't be available for ten years, so their needs to be a way to fill the shortfall. First, Aaron wants to make sure John understands what the shortfall is. The list of income on the whiteboard is:

Rent..*$150,000.00*
401(k)–$500,000..*$20,000.00*
Other investments–$500,000............................*$20,000.00*
Total able to spend at retirement....................*$190,000.00*
Retirement spending need..............................*$300,000.00*
Initial shortfall...*$110,000.00*

John frowns. He isn't happy with Aaron's calculation. *Aaron must be wrong.* He looks at the numbers again. He adds them on his calculator. Numbers don't lie. He sighs and turns to Aaron. "Ann was right; we do have work to do if we're going to be able to afford the retirement we want. I see that we're going to have to work on this how-much-I-need step. We either need to find a way to increase our cash or reduce our spending. Or both. I'm sure we could reduce our spending, but I'm not sure we want to. This could be a problem."

Aaron knows how depressing this information can be. He's had to deliver this kind of bad news before. "I've seen this situation with dozens of other business owners I've worked with. I'm confident we'll be able to work out some ways for you to solve this issue." Aaron leans forward, rests an elbow on the chair arm. "If you're going to transfer your business to your children, you and Ann are going to have to come to grips with the fact that a pretty good chunk of your retirement will have to come from the business after you leave it. We're going to have to put some things in place that will protect you and Ann after you leave, and those protections are easier to put in place than you think. But before we get into those protections, let's move on to the next step of leaving your business."

Aaron goes back to the whiteboard. He writes *Step #2: What's Your Business Worth?*

"Before we can figure out what your business is worth, we need to take a step or two back. Your business lives in what Rob Slee calls 'value worlds.' In fact, your business has at least five values right now as we speak. You might sell it for any number of different asking prices, depending on the buyer."

John's confused, angry even. "The price is the price. Why would the value be different?"

"The truth is every private business, including yours, has several values at the same time. For example, if you were to liquidate your business, that would be one value, probably one you wouldn't like. Then, at the other end of the spectrum are the tech companies in Silicon Valley. They live in what's called the 'intellectual capital value' world. This value is like outer space; it's where the buyer is interested in scaling the company's intellectual capital and really doesn't care about current cash flow. They're paying for possibilities.

"Now, between the unlikely liquidation value and the intellectual capital value lie three or four other realistic values for your business—a spectrum of sorts. Because you want to transfer your business to your children, the value of your business will end up being at the low end of the possible business values spectrum. If you were to sell it to a private equity group or a competitor, the value would be on the upper end. These two sales methods are called a financial sale and a strategic sale."

John has to think about this for a second. He wants his kids to own the business, and he wants to be financially independent. It almost seems like both of these wants are opposed to each other. "Why would I get less money from my kids than anyone else?"

"That's simple. A buyer will only pay you what they can afford to pay and what they think the number is that can net them a positive return. If you sold your business to a competitor, it would be called a strategic sale. They would make your overhead go away, and as a result of that, they could afford to pay you more money.

"If you sell your business to a financial buyer, like a private equity firm, they'll have outside capital they can afford to put into the company as a down payment, and they'd likely borrow the rest of the money from a bank. They can also afford to pay you more.

"When it comes to your family buying the business, they have no outside capital, so they'd have to use you as their bank. That's why when we put together the actual deal, we're going to have to be very careful that we protect you and Ann above anything else. We also have to make sure you can afford to sell the business to your kids. This means the proceeds you get from the business sale have to be enough for you and Ann to retire comfortably. This will require that the company make more money, which makes it worth more. Whether this is done or not will be the responsibility of Alicia and the management team. If they build the value, which I think they will, that's good, but if not, we need to have a plan B.

"If you remember back to the four-box exercise we just did, right now there isn't enough money available for your financial needs. You also should take note that you'll be leasing your building to your children. That lease income will also be a part of your retirement. That income will be entirely dependent on your children successfully running the company after you leave."

That is a lot for John to take in. He feels as if he's being fed from a fire hose. He gets up and paces nervously around the office. He isn't looking forward to his conversation with Ann this evening.

CHAPTER 8

Meeting Everyone's Needs

● ● ●

After a much-needed break, the two men pick up where they left off. John has had plenty of time to think. Instead of feeling a sense of clarity, he's more nervous than before.

"Aaron, do you think you'd be willing to have this conversation with Ann and me? I know I'm going to need to hear it again, and I want Ann to understand what it could mean for us if we sell the business to the kids."

Selling the business to the kids is now an 'if' for John; not a certainty. Aaron asks, "What's changed here for you?" He knows he doesn't have to clarify the question.

"I never thought about the risk. I love my kids, both of us do… but I think we need to keep our options open. Ann would have to agree with that." He runs a hand through his hair. "Sure, Alicia should be able to take on the business, but she's not proven that yet. I have no idea how to talk with her about that. And I especially don't want to have this conversation with Adam. Like I need that grief."

Aaron has never relished telling his clients what *could* happen if they transferred their business to either their children or managers, that there are certain risks involved, but it has to be done. He also knows that there are some easy ways to lessen the risk.

The most important question for Aaron is whether Alicia could take over and run the company. He agrees with John's assessment. She isn't ready yet that much is for sure, but she could do just fine with proper training and navigating a few challenges.

Like John, he's worried about Adam's reaction to the news that the business might not be sold to him and his sister. That is, if Adam's even part of the picture.

"Look, your situation isn't unique. Most of the time, the internal transfer to family works out fine. There've been a few exceptions, of course. And there have been a variety of reasons we decided selling the business to an outsider was the better option. That being said, we're likely going to want to organize a family meeting to go over the options and the associated risks.

"We also have to focus with your management team, come up with a plan to increase the value of the business and improve the cash flow so you and Ann don't have to lower your standard of living and the kids can afford to pay you out. For an internal sale, I believe the approximate value of your business is about $2,000,000 today. I think we need to increase that by almost 50%. That means we need to improve your cash flow by about $200,000 per year. I also believe that this would be a very doable goal for your management team."

Aaron wants to get through the rest of the eight steps. He needs to pick up the pace. Now it's time to move to increasing the value of the business. He writes this on the whiteboard: *Step #3: Increasing the Value of the Business.*

"Before you can walk away from your business, we'll need to further increase its value. Part of that will entail looking at how money is being used at Aardvark. Then we'll want to put together strategies that will increase your cash flow. I'm going to suggest that we include your management team in this step."

Aaron continues, "When we go down the road of an internal transaction, with rare exceptions, we need to improve the value of the business for the selling owner. Most owners think their business is worth way more than it is, and we have to overcompensate for this misperception. Then we need more cash available for retirement."

Aaron pauses to make sure John is tracking him. He can tell by John's slouched posture that he's heard every unwelcome word. "Often, I have to give bad news to owners. I've got to tell them that in order to improve the value, they're going to need to keep running the business for a few years more than they originally wanted to. But there's a silver lining. In many cases, we can create a business that's way more fun to run. Half the time, the owner never wants to leave."

John takes that information in. Working for a few more years isn't the worst thing that can happen. John loves what he does, and he really doesn't have anything better to go to. He upgraded his management team and saw that the company seemed to run better and better as he backed off from day-to-day operations. His life became far more manageable. A thought occurred to him. "How much information do you plan to share with my managers?"

John is concerned about information sharing. It's something he and Aaron never get on the same page about. Aaron keeps trying to convince him that sharing more information is better than sharing less. John's problem is he just doesn't buy it, even though transparency has worked out for him in the recent past.

John is willing to allow Aaron to let the managers in on the secret that he needs more money to retire. It makes sense for his managers to know. At least they'll understand why he's driving for more profit. John always worries that his employees think he's running the company just for his own benefit, and that's what's at the core of his not wanting to share information with anyone, much less his managers.

Feeling a little stiff, Aaron walks over to the window. He turns around, leans against the sill, and crosses his arms. "I was planning on telling them precisely where you stood financially. Which would have to happen anyway for an internal transition to your children to become a reality. I don't plan on talking about the other options available to you. They're smart people. They'll figure that out for themselves. If asked, however, I plan to give them an honest answer. Is that OK with you?"

John doesn't see any other options. He slowly nods yes. "I'm nervous. If they smell trouble, who knows what they'll do."

Aaron chuckles. He knew this was coming. Most of his clients share this worry. "When we get to step five, I'll go into why your key people won't leave you in the lurch. In fact, I've never seen that happen as long as we've been transparent and let people know what's going on sooner rather than later.

"The only time I've seen key people bail is when we waited too long to bring them into the planning. Then they thought we were trying to hide things from them. I'm assuming this is something you don't want to happen."

"Like I'd want that to happen?" John feels his temper rising. "I'll leave it to you to know how to have the conversation with the managers. I get that we have to increase the value of the company, and I understand why. I'm just curious what magic trick we're going to use to get this done. I thought we'd already improved all the areas we can improve."

Aaron laughs. "Improving profits, systems, and innovation is a never-ending process. Let's put this aside for the time being so we can get through the rest of the steps."

It's John's turn to stretch. "What's next?" he asks, leaning against his desk.

"This is where we figure out who's going to buy the business." He writes on the whiteboard: *Step #4: Who Will Buy the Business?* "As you're well aware, everyone is concerned with this. You're concerned because of your desire to keep the company going, to have it live beyond you, preferably under the guidance of one of your children. Ann is concerned for two reasons. She wants to make sure there's enough money for retirement and a future for Adam. Your managers are concerned because they don't know who will take over from you, if the transition will be acceptable or not. And finally, Alicia wants to know if she'll wind up running the place or not."

This is the step John is most concerned with. It's the very issue that caused him to pick up the phone and call Aaron again. This is the question that has to be answered. "I'd love to have Alicia take over if she has the ability and we can afford to have her do so."

John speaks slowly. He tries to find the right words. "Having Alicia take over would likely fit in with everyone's expectations, with the possible exception of Adam. I have no idea what he expects or even wants. I'm hoping your conversation with him will shed some light on this. Although, I don't think you're going to get anywhere there. I'm betting he has no idea. He probably wouldn't answer you straight if he did. He might just have to go along with what his mother and I decide."

John picks up a squeeze toy from the desktop, tosses it back and forth. "I'm worried that Alicia isn't ready to take over. I'm not even sure what she needs to do to get ready. She doesn't have a technical background. She doesn't really understand innovation and planning. Sure, she's done a great job at marketing, but that's just a small part of what she needs to know. It would take her at least three years, if not longer, to learn all the stuff she needs to know."

Aaron listens intently. He knows what Alicia needs, but he's more interested in getting through all eight steps and tying them together before lunch. John isn't done thinking out loud about his concerns.

"I'd like to have Alicia take over the company. But after what we talked about, Ann and I are going to need to understand the options so we can make the best decision for us. I love my kids, you know, and I want them to have the best. I'm sure I don't need to tell you that. But I've also spent thirty-some-odd years running this company and want to make sure Ann and I are comfortable after I retire."

Aaron thinks this is a reasonable way to look at the situation. "Let's table this concern until you, Ann, and I can get together and talk about options. With your permission, I'll move on to number five."

He writes on the whiteboard: *Step #5: Keeping Key Players Through the Transition.*

"This is the step where we make sure Janice, George, and your other managers stay through a transition. This is also where we help them understand that their jobs will be safe, and if they're not, how, precisely, you're going to protect them for a certain amount of time."

John scratches his head. "How am I supposed to make sure my key people are taken care of? I'm not even sure who's going to be the next owner of the company. Take Janice. She wants this to be her last job. She has about ten years left before she retires. If Alicia takes over in four or five years, where does that leave Janice? How can I guarantee that Alicia won't let her go? She already thinks she can do Janice's job."

"Those are all good questions." Aaron has witnessed the strong relationship between Janice and Alicia. He's not worried. "They'll all have to be answered before you transition the business. We can talk with your people about your intentions. I know this sounds like a repeating record; you'll probably need to be a little more transparent than you're comfortable being. Being transparent is necessary if we want to have a smooth transition."

Aaron thinks this would be a good time to introduce a concept that's key to this part of the succession strategy. "Have you ever heard of a stay bonus?"

John shakes his head no.

"It's a pretty simple thing, really. New owners want to make sure they have the current management team during a transition, right? It just makes their lives much easier. This is true for an internal transition to family or managers, or an external one to an outside buyer. The stay bonus is something that kicks in if there's a substantial change of ownership. Essentially, those who are eligible for the stay bonus will get a bonus of six months of their salary if they stay with the new owners for at least one year."

John adds up the amount in his head—three key managers at six months a piece. A stay bonus would be very expensive. No buyer in his right mind would pick up the cost. "Even Alicia wouldn't pay for that."

Aaron raises a finger. "If you were to get an extra $2,000,000 for your business, would you be willing to give your key people, what, $400,000?"

"Yeah, sure, but how is that going to happen, especially if Alicia is the buyer?"

"I can tell you that having a stay bonus in place will increase the value of your business if you have either an inside or outside buyer. An outside buyer will have no further interest in you once they take over the business. An inside buyer will need the support of your senior team if they're to be successful."

Aaron taps the whiteboard. "If Alicia is the buyer, there's a good chance we can get her to pick up the cost of the stay bonus. There are some relatively easy things she can do to that end. Regardless, coming up with enough money for a stay bonus is just one more reason we need to improve the cash flow in the business. We're going to need excess cash to make this plan work.

"If we use the plans I'm going to recommend, including the one to fund a stay bonus, I can almost guarantee that Alicia will enthusiastically go along with what we suggest. It'll cost her some money, but in the end, she'll get a great return on the investment. That's something she's going to need to learn about. She's going to need to spend time with both Jack, the controller, and your accountant to understand the financial impact of any decision she makes."

Aaron looks at his watch. He knows they need to push on, and he also knows that if he doesn't give John a short break, nothing he says will stick.

CHAPTER 9

Thinking Like An Investor, Not A Business Owner

● ● ●

Five minutes later, John and Aaron reconvene in John's office. A breath of fresh air and a splash of water across the face have done each of them good.

Aaron hits the whiteboard again and writes: *Step #6: Protect Your Asset.* The marker squeaks at the last word. "Let's move on to what it's going to take to protect your asset. I'm not only talking about your cash and investment assets; I'm also talking about making sure Alicia pays you what you're owed. The sales price is the asset we're concerned with. We'll also look at what protections you'll need if you sell your business to a third party."

John thinks he understands this part. "We need to make sure that any promises made when I sell are kept throughout the payout process. I understand we need to protect my financial assets. I have no idea what you mean by making sure that Alicia pays me what she owes me. You're telling me that my own kids would screw me?"

Aaron puts the marker on the sill and raises a finger. "You're going to be the bank. You need to act like a bank. That means you'll have language in your sales agreement that allows you to take over the company if she doesn't maintain certain financial benchmarks. Alicia will also have to personally guarantee the loan she has with you. You want her to really feel like she has skin in the game."

John takes this in, feels the weight of the message.

"Here's the bottom line. You really won't be giving up total control of the company until you're fully paid out. You might sell the company to Alicia in four and a half years. You might have to wait another ten years until you're fully paid out. Maybe you never step foot in the office once Alicia takes over. But you will need the ability to step in if things go badly. That's how you protect your asset."

"Now, how do I do that?" John is interested in the how-to, but he can also imagine the outrage his daughter would express if he stepped back in.

"The easiest way is to have what's called covenants in the loan agreement with whoever buys the company. If those covenants are breached, you would have the opportunity to take back your collateral just like a bank. Unlike a bank, you'll have the right to vote all the company stock, which means you could replace the board of directors and take any steps necessary to correct the business.

"This is not something you're going to want to do. It's something you'll need to have available to you should you need it.

"If you're going to be the bank, act like a bank. That means anyone who buys the business from you must realize this is a business transaction. Even if that someone happens to be a family member."

John likes where this part of the conversation is going. He didn't think he would, but he does. Ann will take a bit of convincing until she understands the financial ramifications of what would happen when the business is sold. "That all sounds good to me. Like everything else, we're going to have to fully explain what we're doing and, more importantly, why to Ann."

Aaron is impressed. This engagement is moving along much more smoothly than the last time, thanks to the trust he and John have built. Last time, Aaron had to spend a lot of time and energy justifying his every recommendation. This time he's able to go back to values, questions, and trust to help things move along smoothly.

With two more topics to cover, Aaron moves on. He writes on the whiteboard: *Step #7: Investing the Proceeds.*

The idea of investing the proceeds from the sale of the business is always an attractive one for his clients. All that money hitting the bank account at one time is a vision they are more than happy to entertain. The issue, however, is coming up with the portion they actually get to spend. There's a big difference between cash flow when you're running a business and cash flow when you've sold it. Business owners are used to spending the cash their business produces. Once they sell the business, however, they get much less that they can spend.

Aaron goes over the numbers. If John got $2,000,000 for his business, he couldn't spend that in one year. First, he'd need to pay taxes, which would add up to about $400,000. He'd then be left with $1,600,000. He couldn't spend all of that in one year or he'd go broke. Instead, he could spend about 4% of that value, which would amount to about $64,000 per year. Since he lives on $300,000 per year, he would naturally think that the business, when it's sold, should produce much more money for him. Aaron drives home the message that it won't.

Aaron continues. "Let's spend just a few minutes on investing the money you'll be getting from the sale of your business. To be more accurate, let's talk about how we're going to create the cash that you and Ann will live on once you retire."

John frowns. He thinks he will be able to spend a lot more money. He's slowly realizing that the value of his business in retirement will be much less than he thought it would be.

Aaron continues, "Let's go back to our four-box exercise. You saw that your business was actually going to be worth less on cash flow, meaning what you can spend every year than your business. The most valuable asset you have for retirement is the building. And, as I've said before, both of those assets depend on how well Alicia will run the business."

"Let's start thinking about the allocation of the investment money you have and will have.

"The investments are the tricky part. We need to make sure you never have to worry about how you're invested. This means we need to manage how much of your investments are allocated to stocks, fixed income like bonds and cash. We use a system that's called the bucket system. This is another bucket system, not the one we used to calculate the necessary retirement income.

"Typically, the bucket system looks like this."

Aaron heads back to the couch and takes out his yellow pad again. He flips the page and draws three buckets. He then labels each bucket, one for cash, one for fixed income, and one for stocks. Finally, he writes numbers over each column. Over the cash bucket he writes three years, over the fixed income he writes seven years, and over the stocks bucket he just writes all of the rest.

John looks at the legal pad, turning his head this way, then that. "OK, I'll bite, what are these columns and what do the numbers mean?"

"The cash bucket is how many years of cash you need to have available on a yearly basis. This isn't the total amount of money you spend, just what you need in cash. The fixed income bucket is how many years of bonds and other fixed investments. And then the rest of the money goes into stocks and equity-like investments. The other key here is that we actually want to have three different investment accounts so you can see how the balances fare in both good and bad times.

"Let's walk through an example. Let's say you have $3,000,000 in assets when you retire. Let's also keep with the $300,000 that you'll need to live on. This means that the first year you retire, you're going to need about $325,000, which is adjusted for inflation. Over half the money you need to live on will come from the rent of your building. Remember, we're keeping that separate from the sale of the business. You'll also get about $40,000 per year in Social Security. So, you've got a total of $190,000 in cash flow, which means you'll then need an additional $135,000 in income from other sources to fill your lifestyle needs.

"Looking at our buckets again... If you need three years of cash, that's how much we need to place in this bucket; we've got to put $400,000 in the bucket. That's three years of cash at $135,000. The additional amount, as I already said, will come from rent and Social Security."

Aaron points to the next bucket with his pen. "Then we'll be buying fixed income investments of seven years of about $950,000. That's seven years at that same $135,000 per year amount." He then points to the third bucket. "That leaves a balance of $1,650,000 in assets that you'll place in stock accounts."

John studies the numbers. Any way he looks at it, that much cash and fixed investments seems like way too much. He waits for Aaron's explanation, which he knows is coming.

Aaron continues. "My experience with you and Ann is that both of you are pretty conservative when it comes to your money.

"I want you to stay comfortable through all sorts of market trends. If the stock market is strong and growing, you'll take the income you need from your stock accounts. If the stock market is down, you'll first take money out of fixed income. You can do that for a number of years because you've got seven years' worth of money and the income it throws off. If we happen to have a depression, then you have cash as a backup. The key here is to keep you invested in stocks, whether they're up or down. I've found that using three separate accounts will help you be comfortable with where your money is and have a reasonable, well, more reasonable, chance that you won't be selling stocks when they're down in value."

John gets the basic gist. He'll understand it better when Aaron repeats the breakdown to Ann.

"Can we move on to the last item?" Aaron asks. He gets back up and writes the following on the whiteboard: *Step #8: What Comes Next?* Then he pauses for a bit. He wants to get a few things across to John, and he has to make it as simple as possible. John's a smart man, but this is a stressful situation. Stress slows the brain way down. That and almost every business owner he's ever worked with has a hard time understanding why the what-comes-next question would pose a problem.

Of course, they knew what came next. They'd do all of the things they wanted to do but never got around to doing. When Aaron asks them what that might be, more often than not, they'd tell him that they'd play golf every day. Aaron knows that if that was their only answer, there will be some real problems.

Aaron knows that if he doesn't get this part of the transition right, there will be a good chance it won't happen at all. This is especially dangerous when working on an internal transaction. It never worked out well when the retiring owner looked at his future, didn't like what he saw and then decided not to transfer the business after all. When this happens, all sorts of problems occur. Aaron wants to make sure this doesn't happen to John and his family.

Aaron starts in. "The last and I think the most important thing for you to answer is what's going to be next in your life. This is the main concern Ann has. If you remember, she told me she had a full life, and fitting you into it would be a challenge. You've made a life for yourself here. Now, you have to make a life for yourself separate and apart from the business."

John is under no illusions. This is going to be hard for him. He hasn't admitted it to Ann yet, but he knows it's the truth.

"I want you to first understand that leaving your company is a major transition. It's something that's going to take time, and there'll likely be some pain along the way.

"The Financial Transitionist, Susan Bradley, discovered that there are four areas of transition. It's a model I love and use all of the time when it comes time to leave your business.

"The first stage is anticipation. This is where an owner would think about and anticipate the sale of their business." Aaron knows this stage can often last for as many as twenty or thirty years. It's the major difference between a business transition and any other variety. In most other transitions, the time frame for anticipating a major change is much shorter.

Aaron remembers he has a great graphic that shows the four stages and pulls it out of his briefcase. "I want you to take a look at this graphic. These are four stages of transition that happens when business owners leave their business."

He goes on to point out that the second stage is ending. This part of the transition is when an ending takes place. This would be the day John transfers the business to Alicia and steps out of both operations and strategy.

The third and most difficult stage is passage. This is the messy part. John will have times when he's likely depressed. He'll find that many of his business contacts disappear, not because they don't like him, but because he's off the radar screen.

Finally, we get to the new normal. This is like a butterfly leaving its cocoon; John will emerge from the challenges and upset of selling his business into having a fulfilling life once again, one with different interests. He might even wonder how he's become so busy again.

"I spend a lot of time working with selling business owners on these four stages. I used to believe that I could help people like you avoid seller's remorse. I no longer believe that. Now, I believe I can help you manage and move through it. You're going to feel some pain and loss. It's just part of the deal. There are also specific things you'll need to be doing while we're getting ready for the transition to happen."

John feels the pressure. "What can you do to help? Because I need this to go smoothly. For everybody's sake."

"For example, as Alicia or whoever is the next CEO of the company gets ready to take over, you and Ann will start spending more and more time away from the business. You might decide to travel, you might decide to learn a new skill. Whatever it is that you decide to do, the first week you won't call in at all. The second period will be for two weeks. In the year that you transfer the business, we're going to want you to spend at least six months away and never call the business. You'll get a real flavor of what leaving the business is about and how your life will be different.

"Lots of owners have a hard time with this. I can tell you that by starting with a small amount of time away from the business and then expanding the amount of time you're away, you'll find that when the day actually comes, yes, you'll miss your business. Working up to leaving will be much less devastating than if you just go cold turkey, leave your business, and never come back again."

John looks out the window and slumps in his chair. He knew the day would eventually come, and he really wasn't looking forward to it. He loves working at Aardvark. For the most part, he's no longer involved much in the day-to-day operations and can do what he likes. He wonders whether he really wants to go down this road.

CHAPTER 10

The Manager's Meeting

● ● ●

By now, Aaron knows his way around the plant despite Aardvark being a very different place than it was six years ago.

Six years ago, when he navigated the plant, no one would look at him, much less look him in the eye. Now, not only do people look at him, but they smile and say hello. This is just one more reminder that the atmosphere in the company has greatly improved. It also tells him that the managers have done a great job of living the values the company holds.

Aaron thinks back to the challenge he had getting John to even think about values, much less implement them. Now he can see them being used.

He easily finds the conference room where he is scheduled to meet with the full management team. He stands at the door before entering the room. On the wall are the values and the clarifying statements. He notices that some of the statements have changed slightly since the last time he was there. This is excellent news. That means the values are living and breathing, and not just something stuck on some wall.

Aaron enters the conference room, looks around, and says hello. He goes over to the side table, grabs a water, a sandwich, and a salad. And, as usual, he takes a seat in the middle of the table. Janice is at the head of the table with George and Alicia on either side of her. Jack Cole, the controller, is sitting at the opposite end of the table, slumped over. Finally, there's Stan Sockitt, the sales manager who, from the disinterested look on his face, isn't sure why he's even in the meeting.

Aaron studies the body language of each person at the table. Jack looks to be expecting the worst, given his darting eyes. Aaron thinks he should begin by addressing Jack to draw him into the group and help him feel more comfortable. Everyone else seems open and ready for the conversation.

"Jack, how are things?"

Jack mumbles, "I guess they're OK. Well, from the outside, they're OK. I have to think that, because you're here, they probably aren't. Otherwise, why would you show up?"

Aaron bets there are other people in the room thinking the very same thing. "That's a reasonable concern. If I were in your shoes, I might even be thinking the same thing. I'm here to help John and Aardvark come up with a succession strategy for the company. We'll be focusing on transferring the business to the family, and we're not sure what that looks like yet." He notices Alicia shifting in her chair. "I do know that John is committed to seeing that happen. As long as we all work together, everyone will win.

"I do know that there's some work to be done. John and I have come up with ten things that need to be accomplished or satisfied before we can execute a transition plan." Aaron runs through the list of the items and summarizes his take on them. When no one asks any questions, he continues. "I'm going to guess that we'll identify one or two other things we'll need to add to that list during this meeting."

Jack stops slouching. He no longer looks like he's about to hide under the table. Aaron learned during the last go-round that Jack often looked like the world was about to fall apart. That seems to be the typical demeanor of a controller. Like Chicken Little, their role is to warn the owner of impending doom. Jack is no different in that respect.

Aaron addresses the other participants. "I've passed out an infographic I use to help with these conversations. I find that using this model to take us through the process is highly effective. You'll see that accompanying each of the steps of the transition process are the open things that John and Ann have. I call this the road map to a sale ready company. Let's be clear; in our case, a sale ready company does not mean getting the company ready to be sold to an outsider. John has been very clear, and he remains clear that he wants the business to stay in the family. For that to happen, we're going to have to work together as a team.

"You'll find that having a sale ready company is really no different than having an economically and personally sustainable business. It's really two sides of the same coin. The only difference is we're focusing on the transition part for John, and we'll be focusing on the sustainable part for John's children."

Aaron nods at Alicia after he says that.

"I think looking at each of the necessary steps to a sale ready company is a good way to stay focused on what we need to do.

"By the way, the eight steps don't necessarily speak to the order in which we'll go after the issues. I find that we almost always go out of order when we actually do the work. Are there any thoughts about what you're looking at?" Aaron scans each of their faces.

The participants read through the sheet before them. They ask a few clarifying questions about what each step involves.

Stan, however, looks like he's swallowed a frog. He stares at the sheet in front of him. "Aaron, I felt this way last time you were here, and this time is no different. I have no idea why I'm here. What do I have to do with any of this? I'm in sales."

Aaron points at Stan with an open hand. "Who is closer to the customer than anyone else in the room? Who has their ear to the ground? Do you think you might have something to say when we start talking about increasing the value of the company? Because that's the main topic on our agenda."

Stan mumbles. "I guess I might have something to add."

Aaron smiles. "I expect you'll have more than something to add."

He then pivots. "I want to try an experiment with you folks. Last time I was here we focused on the economic and personal sustainability of the company for John. We ended up going past that to the economic and personal sustainability for all the stakeholders of Aardvark. By going past John's needs and including all of the team members here, we expanded our view of what needed to happen. You might remember the four drivers for that outcome included being a values led company, having John become operationally irrelevant, putting together a recurring revenue stream, and then filling the four buckets of profit.

"The four buckets of profit provide, first, a great lifestyle for John. Then, a fully funded emergency fund, a fully funded retirement plan for John, and then a fully funded growth program for the company.

"Some of those profit buckets are now fully funded, John's lifestyle, for instance, and some need work, such as John's retirement plan. Nonetheless, you've made remarkable progress by achieving these outcomes and should be very proud of yourself. And, we have more work to do to create the financial sustainability necessary for a transition."

The managers around the table all nod their heads in understanding. Some even smile, including Jack, the controller. After a beat, Jack goes back to appearing glum.

"Today, we're focusing on the eight steps that lead to a successful transition. This is not as simple an exercise as you might think. The trick is to integrate the eight steps we're about to cover with the things John and Ann want and need so they're comfortable and able to make a successful transition. We're going to need a map for how all these things fit together. And that'll take teamwork and creativity. If you're asking what any of this has to do with us, I'm sure you'll be surprised by the answers you come up with by the end of the meeting."

Janice squirms in her seat. She jumps in. "This sounds interesting, but I'm confused; how do we start?"

Aaron says, "Let's start with values. That's probably easiest."

Janice looks confused, "I thought we were talking about the eight steps that John needs to leave the business. Now we're talking about values. I don't get why we're starting here." She crosses her arms and frowns.

Aaron realizes he missed a major step. He forgot to let the group know that they would be working on what John and Ann need to transfer the business, tie that into the four drivers of sustainability, and lay them over the eight steps of a sale ready company. He also knows this is pretty complicated, and he needs to slow down a little if he wants to have this meeting be a success.

Aaron says, "I apologize. I've not done a good job of setting the agenda for this meeting and what I hope we accomplish. I've given you the eight steps of a sale ready company and the needs and wants that John and Ann have. I didn't let you know that we're going to also integrate our conversation with the four drivers of a sustainable business. For review, they are being a values led company, having a recurring revenue stream, having the owner become operationally irrelevant, and systematizing a company. Let's start the conversation with values."

Janice looks visibly relieved. Aaron can also see the rest of the team looks less confused. He hopes his experiment doesn't go off the tracks and become a wasted hour.

Janice says, "The thing about values is that they've helped us get everyone on the same page. They've helped us to communicate about what it is we do internally and with our customers. I would say we're well on our way to becoming a values led company. Being values led has made us a better company, and that automatically helps us increase the value of the business.

"I've also seen that the more we use our values as tools, the easier it is for us to manage and talk about what's important here."

Aaron says, "That could have been me talking. I don't think I could have said that any better myself."

George studies the two lists before him. "It looks to me like being values led also works for protecting the assets for both the family and its employees. There's less chance of the place blowing up because we don't know what we're supposed to be doing. That is, with the exception of one person."

By the way the managers refuse to look at Aaron, it's clear that everyone understands George's reference. Aaron needs to keep everyone focused on the agenda at hand, not on Adam, so he launches ahead. He decides to ignore George's last comment.

"OK, let's talk about the next requirement for Aardvark's financial sustainability: having John become operationally irrelevant in the business. This was important before; it's even more important now. Why?"

This time Jack talks first. "I have to say that John has stopped being the bottleneck in the company. Having a dashboard in place where he can see what's going on has made my life a lot easier. The problem is getting John to look at it on a regular basis. He ignores it when things are going well, and if there's a hiccup, he still goes a little bit crazy. If we're talking about being economically sustainable, then keeping him operating in his own lane will allow us to do our jobs without him getting in the way."

Stan also has something to say. "With John out of the picture for the most part, our customers have stopped asking me who is going to replace John and what happens if he gets hit by a bus. Also, having Alicia in the picture gives our customers the sense that there's a successor around who'll eventually take over. I think this helps make our customers confident of continuity in our business and will continue to do so."

For the first time, Alicia speaks up. "I can say one thing. My dad seems to be happier. I think he likes what he's doing now. Don't get me wrong, that's great, but… This has nothing to do with increasing the value of the company, which is what we're all talking about." She seems to look for her words. "But that might be a problem when it comes time for him to move on. I'm looking at the eight steps here, and I can see a big sticking point. I'm a little afraid he's going to decide the business is a better option than what he's got in front of him."

Aaron is impressed with Alicia's insight. He can see why she's John's favorite. He can also see why Ann might have a problem with her, why she might protect Adam and assume he's getting short shrift.

"Like I said," Aaron says to Alicia, "we're not going to be taking these steps in order. We'll see the problems that promise to arise in one step as we're working through another. Your father and I have already talked about that. It's one of the things on the list to be dealt with before he can walk away from the business. We're on it.

"Let's move on to the next factor in a sustainable business. A recurring revenue stream. Does that fit in with the eight steps anywhere? Where does a recurring revenue stream promise to affect John's ability to walk away from the company?"

Placing a finger on the paper before him, Jack speaks up again. "Well, it certainly fits in with what the business is worth and increasing the value of the business. If we can get more repeat orders, we'll have a more attractive company. That should improve our cash flow."

Jack continues. "We need to think about not only doing prototype work for our customers but also the production runs when they go into full production. I wonder if partnering with a bigger company might make sense?"

Aaron says, "Stan? Any thoughts?"

Stan answers, "I'd rather see us work with fewer accounts and do both the prototype work that we're great at and then move them to full production with us. If we do that, we'll need to prove we have the capability of providing both services."

Aaron loves where this conversation is going. He also knows that his conversation with Adam is right around the corner, and he needs to keep the meeting moving forward.

Aaron says, "Those are great ideas. I'd love the management team to work on them. Since we're short on time, we're going to have to keep going; I'll leave it to you to work on these ideas a little later.

"OK, let's dive into the last driver of sustainability: systems. How does that factor in with what we're talking about?"

Janice speaks up. "When we were on the buy side, and I'm talking about the other companies I worked at, if the seller didn't have great systems, we would take a pass. We weren't interested in educating a bunch of employees. We knew that when we bought a company, we would tweak their systems, which is so much easier than trying to implement from scratch.

"Having great systems will increase the business' value. And quite possibly, influence who's going to buy it. Assuming, of course, that John doesn't transfer the business to the family." She glances at Alicia. "I hate to say this, but the better our systems are, the more attractive we become to outside companies. It might be difficult for John to turn down the big numbers that would likely come his way if he put the company up for sale to an outsider."

Aaron wishes Janice had kept quiet on the topic of the company being attractive to outsiders. He can see Alicia seething. The room goes silent. Everyone is still.

Alicia now appears to be on the verge of tears. The rest of the team grows nervous. Aaron knows he needs to do something and do something now. He says, "It's true that having great systems makes a company attractive to a third party. The conversation John and I have had about transferring the business has been about him having enough to live on after exiting the business. We've talked about selling to a third party, and he told me he only plans to do this if he can't get enough money for retirement by doing an internal transition.

"That's why I wanted to have this meeting with all of you. John's ability to transfer the business is really up to the work that all of you do. John is not looking to maximize the amount of money he gets when he leaves the business. He's looking to have enough, and the difference between the two is huge."

Alicia releases an audible sigh. Aaron hopes she's getting her arms around how difficult a decision this is for her father. Aaron knows this is not the way he would like to share John's options with her. At the same time, by the look on her face, it got her attention. Aaron decides to clean this up later.

Glancing at the clock, he says, "Let's move on to the last item, and that's the four buckets of profit. As we all know, this is a result and not a driver of a sale ready company. It helps us measure our success.

"Jack, you're the money man. Do you have any thoughts on this?"

Jack rubs his chin, slips lower into his chair while he thinks. When he's ready to speak, he sits up again. "It seems to me that we're doing pretty well, but it might not be good enough for John to have enough money for retirement. He still focuses on plowing all of the profits and free cash back into the business and hasn't paid enough attention to himself. I've talked with him about looking at retirement plan options that can put more money into his pocket, and we just never seem to get around to it. And we definitely don't have the extra cash to fund more retirement savings for him."

Aaron speaks up. "Who wants to let us know why we need to focus on filling all the profit needs of the company and John? George, I know you're new here, why don't you give it a shot."

George shoots Aaron a dirty look. Aaron kicks himself for putting George into an uncomfortable situation. He forgets how awkward these conversations are if you haven't seen them play out in front of you a few times. Aaron thinks about having someone else take on the question, but before he can, George starts talking.

"Well, I would think that this profit thing would definitely work into what John needs. For that matter, it really fits in with what all of us need. It might even be something that we're going to need for our key people."

"Alicia, what are your thoughts?" Aaron asks.

"I know my father needs a certain amount of money, and we need to figure out how to meet that number. My guess is we're not creating enough cash, and we're probably not using our cash in the best way. Look, obviously this is important to me. I'm all in. I think our best shot is taking waste out of our manufacturing processes."

Aaron wants to tie the meeting up.

"This was a great exercise, and I thank all of you for participating in it. I know John is counting on all of you to be major players in getting this plan done and allowing him to leave the company in four and a half years. If we do this correctly, everyone should be happy with the outcome. I would love to keep going, but I have time set aside for Adam, and I don't want to be late."

CHAPTER 11

Aaron's Conversation with Adam

● ● ●

Aaron thinks the meeting with the managers went better than he expected. He isn't so sure about how the upcoming conversation with Adam will go. If he is honest with himself, he'd connect with the feeling that he's not looking forward to the conversation. In fact, he's dreading it. And yet, unless there's some resolution to what he calls the Adam issue, there's never going to be a succession plan that will satisfy everyone.

Aaron suspects that Adam is dreading the meeting as well. Probably even more than Aaron.

Even though John has arranged to vacate his office so Aaron can meet with Adam, Aaron isn't sure that's the best place for the meeting to take place. He decides the best action will be for Adam to make that decision. That would force Adam to engage his brain and, hopefully, provide a pattern interruption of sorts. Aaron bets that most people never let Adam lead with a decision. Giving him a choice may give Adam pause.

When Aaron walks into John's office, he finds Adam already there leaning against the far wall. He studiously avoids any eye contact with Aaron. Aaron does the best he can by looking at Adam with what he hopes is a soft, non-judgmental look. "Hi Adam, how're you doing today?"

Adam reels around with both his arms tightly clutching his chest. "What do you care?" He looks like a cornered animal.

Aaron isn't surprised at all. "Well, that might be a good question, but I have a different one for you. Would you like to talk here or would you rather go someplace else?"

Adam sighs. "I don't care. I'm not sure why we're even talking. And frankly, I think you're a fraud and a complete waste of time."

It's Aaron's turn to sigh. He sits down. Crosses his leg. "Then we might as well talk here. Why don't you find a place to sit?"

Adam throws himself into a chair, shoots a dirty look at Aaron, and waits. He seems determined to make this conversation difficult.

"Adam, do you have any idea why we're talking today?"

"Why in the hell would you think I knew or cared?"

If possible, Adam slumps even lower in his chair. From the look of him, he's waiting for a nasty response.

Aaron knows that when such behavior shows itself, his conversation partner is usually drowning in self-pity. Aaron thinks it would be best if he just ignored Adam's aggressive displays and tendencies, pretend they didn't happen. In the past, he found that the tenor of the conversation would change after fifteen or twenty minutes. He hopes that'll happen here.

"Do you know why your father brought me back to Aardvark?"

Adam frowns. "Why would I care? It has nothing to do with me."

"That's where you'd be wrong. It has lots to do with you. In fact, it has lots to do with everyone in your family.

"The reason I'm back is because your father wanted my help with putting together a succession plan. He's not sure how he wants to leave the business, who he wants to leave it to, or if he'll be able to leave it at all. We're going to work on all three of those things."

Adam's posture doesn't tell Aaron if he's getting through. In a very low voice, Adam reveals what he's thinking. "It doesn't matter what you and my father cook up. I'm going to be left out in the cold, totally screwed. You know he's just going to give the whole thing to my sister, and she'll freeze me out. Neither of them cares two bits about me."

Aaron isn't surprised Adam feels this way. "Do you really think that's true? And if so, is that something you want to have happen?"

"I've spent eleven years here, and I'm going to be tossed out without any place to go or any place to work. I know it, and so do you. No one in my family cares a bit about me. It's always Alicia did this wonderful thing, or Alicia is so smart. It's always about her and never about me. I don't care what you or anyone else says, I know I'm going to get screwed."

Aaron arches his eyebrows. "What makes you believe that?"

"You've seen them. They're always criticizing what I do, and they're always trying to put me down. Alicia with her fancy college degrees."

"So, you'll be left behind?"

Adam hesitates. "Well, isn't it obvious? You see the way they act toward me?"

Aaron smiles gently. There's no getting through to anyone who tells themselves the kind of story Adam's telling himself, but he'll try. "Do you think you have anything to do with the way they respond to you?"

Adam shoots Aaron a dirty look. "See, you're already taking their side. I'm not even sure why I'm sitting here talking to you. You know nothing about me." It appears he's so angry, he's practically spitting his words.

Aaron recalls a book he read almost forty years earlier. In the book, there was a section that was called "games we play to keep from losing the game." It was clear to Aaron that Adam's strategy, outlined in this book, was "get them before they get me." It was the same strategy Aaron used whenever he felt he was being backed into a corner.

Aaron rubs his chin and takes a deep breath. "Look, I know you don't want to be here and truthfully, I'm not sure I do either. Do you think we might take it down a notch and see if we can help each other?"

Adam seems perplexed. "You have no interest in helping me." He stumbles over his words. "And anyway, I don't know how you could help me." Adam seems defeated.

Now, Aaron thinks, would be a good time to try and change the conversation. "Look, Adam, I know how tough it is to grow up with someone like your father. I'm going to bet that he was much tougher on you than your sister. I bet he would often demean you about your grades and school. It would be easy to see how you would think he loves your sister way more than you. In fact, most of the time you'd wonder whether he loves you at all.

"I was in a similar situation when I was growing up. My sister was always the well-behaved, smart one. I was the black sheep of my family. I thought about things in a different way and only did things I thought were important. If I didn't think something was important, I ignored it. That got me into more trouble than I ever want to remember. It's tough when your sister gets all of the good attention, and you get all the bad stuff thrown your way."

Adam looks as though he might start crying. "Whatever."

Aaron continues. "I'm going to bet that you often felt dumb and useless."

Adam looks at his shoes.

Aaron knows that hitting too close to home too soon can backfire. He claps his knee. "I've got a question for you. Was there anything you were really good at that you got recognition for?"

In a monotone, Adam says, "Yeah, there was one thing."

Aaron looks at him expectantly.

The young man hesitates. "I've always been good at fixing things. Like, for some reason, I really get machines. I can fix almost anything, and I hardly ever have to look at a manual."

Aaron knows Adam's reputation. He can fix anything. Aaron says, "That's something I definitely can't do. In fact, the saying around our house is that I should never have tools in my hands. They become dangerous there."

Adam looks up. Threatens to laugh.

"Let's get back to you for a while, if that's alright. This might sound like a strange question, but are you happy here?"

Adams nostrils flare. The flicker of amusement drains from his face. "What do you mean am I happy here? What do you think? Do I look happy?"

"Then why stay?"

"What else would I do? I don't have a college degree. I barely even graduated from high school. Who would hire me? No, man, I'm stuck."

It's Aaron's turn to be amused. "You honestly think you couldn't find someplace else to work? Are you kidding? With your skills, you could walk out and find a dozen places to work in less than a week. You might not want to do that, but to say there's no place else to go is just silly."

Adam runs his hands through his hair. Aaron can see he's backing him into a corner. And yet, at least this corner is a different one, one that Adam hasn't been in before. The corner of realizing he has choices, although, at a sub-conscious level, he has to already know he has choices.

Adam shrugs. "Well, maybe I could find another place to work. Fine. At least I wouldn't have to put up with the idiots around here. But then, I'm sure I'd be cut out of the business. My sister would get it all, and I'd be left with nothing. Just like always."

Aaron leans forward, realizing that this is a pivotal part of the conversation. There are two roads he can take the conversation down. Road one, he can guide Adam toward other work opportunities. The other road, having Adam talk about others in the company, will quickly become a "he said, she said" situation. Aaron knows this is a dead-end conversation. He knows he needs to keep the conversation moving forward and away from company gossip or opinions.

"Adam, would you like to spend a little time talking about what having an outside job might look like?" Aaron is curious to see what sort of non-verbal cues Adam is going to give off with this question.

Adam shrugs. "Why should I be the one talking about another job? You know that George is the one who should be the one doing that. I'm an Aardvark and this is our company, not his."

Aaron decides not to take the bait. He can see what George has to deal with when it comes to Adam. Aaron's on to Adam's habit. The young man drops a juicy chunk of bait in the water in the hopes of getting an argument going so no one can pay attention to the real problem. Aaron tucks that piece of information in his hat. He'll want to share that with both George and John. Aaron's sure that if they can find a way to ignore the bait, the relationship between both of them and Adam might get a little better.

Aaron ignores Adam's outburst and just continues as if Adam had asked about his options. "If you were to leave Aardvark, what sort of work would you want to do?"

Adam says, "You're just trying to force me out of here, just like everyone else."

Aaron feels his temper starting to rise. He's been known to have a bad temper, especially when he was younger. Instead of blowing up, he takes several deep breaths and then turns toward Adam. "I know you have no interest in the conversation. I really want to know what you like doing here and how that might let you think about the other options you have. Once again, if you were to leave here, what would you want to do?"

Adam actually thinks about the question for a moment. Aaron isn't sure why. "I know this sounds funny, but I could get into working at a place with metal benders using NC machines. I'm great at programming ours. If I could do that all day, I'd be in heaven. We have way too many old machines here that should have been replaced years ago, and to tell you the truth, I'm sick of fixing them. I'm good at it, don't get me wrong, but it's no fun."

"That's interesting. Would you have any interest in owning a small metal shop?"

"I never thought about it." Adam's eyes narrow. "Wait a minute. What would you get out of it? Is this just my dad's way of getting rid of me? Are you his hatchet man?" He gives Aaron a suspicious look. After Aaron fails to react, he continues. "Anyway, I don't know anything about running a business."

Aaron doesn't take the bait. "I imagine your dad knew nothing about running a business when he started Aardvark."

There's a pause in the conversation. Aaron is closely observing Adam and thinks he sees a small change in his demeanor. He even thinks he sees a slight smile form.

Adam continues. "You know, the funny thing was when I was in school, I aced the stuff I thought would have some usefulness in my life. Most of the stuff those idiots taught was pure garbage. I could run a business if I had to."

Aaron thinks he may have just stumbled across a potential solution for everyone. He's sure Adam has the brains to run a small machine tool shop. If that kid can fix machines the way his father swears he can, the guy's got the goods. Aaron also knows that Aardvark has several sub-contractors in that world. He wonders whether it would make sense for John to help Adam get into business and buy out one of their sub-contractors, if possible.

If this happens, several good things might come out of it. The Adam problem at Aardvark would be solved. They'll need to find another lead maintenance person, sure, but Aaron thinks George is easily up to that task. Ann will likely think that Adam is on a good path with prospects, a positive future. John will only have to worry about who the next owners of the company will be. Alicia won't have to worry about managing the company with her brother getting in the way.

Perhaps this is just the thing that would heal the family.

Adam stares at Aaron, who is lost in his thoughts.

Aaron says, "I've just been thinking about you and a machine shop option. You know, I'm not sure there is much good that can come from you staying here. Not that you couldn't change things around. It would be much easier, and probably cleaner, for everyone involved for you to make a clean break."

Adam maintains a poker face. Aaron can see that he's interested. Adam's breathing has changed, and his body language has subtly softened. He thinks the kid might see a different option.

"There are tons of small machine shops in this part of the world. In fact, many of them have less than ten employees. They can be very specialized, and it would be a great use of your skills. I'm thinking we should have a conversation with your father about this idea. What do you think?"

Adam rubs the back of his neck. "You know, I don't really want to have this conversation with my father. It wouldn't go anywhere. He doesn't think I can do anything useful except fix machines. I'm not sure it'll be worth my time."

Aaron goes still for a minute. "Would you have a problem with me bringing this up to him? Even if he shuts the idea down right away, I think he just might come around to seeing how it's a great solution for all involved. What do you think?"

Adam shrugs. "Knock yourself out. I don't think anything will come of it, but as long as I'm not involved in the ask, do what you want."

Aaron laughs. "Well, that's about the weakest endorsement I've ever heard for an idea. You know, I think you'll be surprised. I think you came up with a great idea. I like it on so many levels. Let's see where it goes."

The ninety minutes that Aaron had allocated to the conversation is up. He thinks it was among the most productive ninety minutes he's ever spent at Aardvark. He now sees the first parts of a great plan coming together.

CHAPTER 12

Dinner with John and Ann

● ● ●

After a catnap at the hotel, Aaron arrives at the restaurant. When he enters, he's glad to find that the tables are well spaced and quiet. This means their conversation will flow; they won't be overheard.

Five minutes later, Ann and John arrive. Aaron gives both a big smile.

Before they even sit down, John looks at Aaron, "So?"

Aaron knows what John is looking for. "Let's sit down, and I'll tell you all about the day. I think it went even better than I expected."

All three head toward their table at the back. John chose this restaurant because he remembered that the last time Aaron had come, he'd complained about their inability to talk in peace. This one will fit the bill, and, on top of it, the food here is top-notch.

In the past five years, John and Ann have become foodies. Part of their increased spending can be tied to them having upgraded the restaurants they frequent.

Everyone settles into his or her chairs. Both Ann and John have questions. It's clear to Aaron that they have yet to talk about what they want to see come out of this dinner because each seems to have their own agenda.

John wants to know what happened with the managers meeting and Aaron's conversation with Adam. He ran into Adam before he went home, and Adam seemed a little less angry for a change. John wonders whether this has anything to do with that conversation.

Ann asks about Adam also. She doesn't have to say a thing for Aaron to know that she's still concerned he's going to find a way to throw Adam out of the company and leave him high and dry. Her body language tells Aaron that she's determined this is not going to happen.

Aaron pauses. He knows he needs to set the tone even before they look at menus. "How about we have a general conversation about Adam and then talk about your retirement?"

Both John and Ann nod in agreement. All three pick up their menus. The waiter comes over for their drink order. After he leaves, Aaron knows it's time to start. "In many respects, my conversation with Adam could have been a conversation I might have had with an outside consultant, back when I was working with my father."

Ann raises an eyebrow.

"I've never told you the story about how I ended up having my own business when I was twenty-four years old. My father and I got along even worse than you and Adam." Aaron knows he has to make sure he keeps his personal history out of the decision-making process at hand. He also knows he needs to share his personal backstory with John and Ann so they understood all of the influences. Aaron wants to make sure he doesn't lead them where he would go and not where they want to go. He says to John, "There was nothing I ever did that was good enough for him. Today, I understand that my father was mostly embarrassed when I made a mistake and took it out on me. This was true of the mistakes I made in school, sports, and most especially when I worked for him."

Ann glances at John, gives him a nudge as if to say, "That sounds exactly like you."

"He was a tough guy." Aaron continues, "One you wouldn't want to get into an argument with. When he really lost his temper, I was always afraid he was going to haul off and take a swing at me. It never happened, but I was always afraid."

John shrugs. He knows he can be tough on Adam. He knows he's fantasized about booting him in the butt. But he would never hurt his son, regardless of how angry he gets. It doesn't matter what it looks like on the outside. It's enough that he knows that's the case.

"Anyway, I was a real punk when I was working for him. I thought I was a genius and everything I did was great. I came across as an arrogant jerk."

With that Ann smiles.

"If you think I can be a bit arrogant today, you've not seen anything. You should've seen me back then.

"About two months after I started working with my dad, he sent me to a location two hours away from our main operation. There was one account that did about $75,000 a year in business, and he had no interest in keeping the account or, more accurately, servicing the account. He wanted me to shut it down as well as the location.

"Instead of getting rid of the account, I added another five new accounts. It was just easy to do. I'm not actually sure why I did it, but it ended up being an important thing for my continuation in that industry. When I came home, my father was both impressed and angry at the same time. How was he supposed to shut down that location now that we had another five accounts that required servicing?

John wants to laugh, but he can't help but appreciate Aaron's father. He hates it when Adam disobeys his orders.

Ann seems enthralled. "What did your father do?"

"He solved the problem by saying, 'I don't want to go up there anymore, so why don't you buy the location from me?'

"And, that's what I did. I bought that one small location from him, and over the next twenty years, turned it into a company with ninety employees."

Buying a small branch from his father was the best thing Aaron ever did. If he had stayed and worked with his father, he would have quit in less than a year. There was no way he and his father would have been able to work together.

The waiter comes by and drops off a breadbasket. He refills the water glasses before walking away, having established that none of them are interested in ordering.

"There were lots of ups and downs along the way, with the downs sometimes being unbelievably painful…" Aaron let his voice trail off. "And yet, it's that experience that kept sneaking into my mind when I was talking with Adam."

"Oh, I don't know," John says. "I don't think you can accuse Adam of being that ambitious. If he wants to rebel, he'd do it in another way."

Ann glares at John, "I have no idea why you continue to be so negative about Adam. He's not a bad kid." Ann turns her face away and stares across the room. In fact, there are times when he's taken lots of initiative. You just won't give him credit for anything, and I'm getting sick of it."

Aaron continues. "There's no question that Adam is a really smart guy. I think both of you agree he can use some work when it comes to emotional intelligence, but his mechanical intelligence and ability to learn when things are applicable to what he's doing are unbelievably high."

John has never thought about Adam as being smart. He knows Adam can fix anything he puts his hands on and makes things run with incredible efficiency. But smart is a different thing.

John thinks back to the times he'd given Adam a hard time as a kid. He never had to talk with him about improvements in science or math. His fights with Adam were always about reading and writing.

Ann leans forward. "Interesting story; don't get me wrong. But what's that got to do with Adam?"

Aaron folds his hands. "That's what I would like to put off for just a little while. I know Adam and his future is number one on your agenda, but I think we need to talk about your financial independence and the options you have before we talk about my idea for Adam. I'm pretty sure that when we get there, you'll like the idea, or at least I hope you will."

Aaron turns to Ann. "Are you willing to let us table my idea about a path for Adam for a few minutes?"

Ann's face relaxes. She nods and settles back against her chair.

The waiter returns with their drinks, and everyone places their order. Aaron is excited. There's duck on the menu, which he orders. Both Ann and John choose their meals. The waiter leaves, and the conversation continues.

"Let's have a conversation about your retirement," Aaron says. He looks at both of them. "There are two things we need to discuss. The first is your finances; the second is how John is going to move out of the company and into his next chapter. I hate that expression, but it more or less fits."

"Next chapter," John says. "That sounds…" He searches for the right word, but nothing comes to him. *Final? Maybe that's it.*

"I'm impressed with how Aardvark is doing. The good news is that you've been able to increase the amount of money you spend on lifestyle by 50%." Aaron waves a hand over the nicely appointed table. "The bad news is that if you were to leave your business today, you would have to cut back on your spending."

Ann turns to her husband. Her face gets red. "You keep telling me we have plenty of money. 'Don't worry,' you say, 'Go ahead and spend the money.'" She turns back to Aaron. "Does this mean we're going to have to go on an austerity budget and change how we live? Because I'm done scraping by. I did that when the kids were little."

John opens his mouth to defend himself. But Aaron holds up his hand in an attempt to calm her. "No, not at all," Aaron says. "It means that we have to talk about your options. I'm not eager to have you cut back on where and how you spend money. That's usually the last resort, and I've never found that to be a useful conversation. I'm simply interested in talking options."

Ann doesn't look so sure.

"Let's start with the good news. John says he wants to be out of Aardvark in about four and a half years. That gives us time to do two things." He raises one finger. "First, we'll be able to help you save more money and, hopefully, a lot more money." He raises the next one. "Second, we can continue making Aardvark more successful, which would give us the ability to get more cash into your pockets."

Ann looks somewhat relieved. "So, you're saying our retirement is going to depend on how well Aardvark does over the next few years?"

"Yes, and with your intended strategy of having the business stay in the family, we need to talk about the risk that comes with banking on the continued success of Aardvark.

"Even after John retires, your financial future will be tied in with the company. Or at least it will with your current plan of having the business stay in the family, with the likelihood that Alicia will be taking over as CEO."

Ann takes a deep breath, "Why do we have to be concerned about Aardvark and whether Alicia can run it, and where does Adam fit in?"

Aaron tells Ann about the challenges of selling to family members and the risk that goes along with it. He knows John also needs to hear this again. Aaron remembers John specifically asked for a repeat of the explanation when they got together with Ann. After the explanation, both seemed to understand that selling to the family came with some personal financial risk for both of them.

So far, John has barely spoken. Hearing Aaron's assessment once again has left him uneasy. He realizes he's taking a significant risk by selling the company to his family. Preference or not, this option is far more complicated than he initially thought. He can practically feel Ann's anxiety level spike through the roof.

John has some business friends who did this with their kids, and after several years, they had to throw the kids out and take over again. This is something he has no interest in seeing play out in his life.

John finally pipes up, "If we sell to the family, how do we protect ourselves?"

Ann adds, "I thought this was going to be easy and not affect our lives."

Aaron spends a few minutes talking about the steps that John and Ann would have to take to protect themselves after John transfers ownership in the business.

Ann listens intently. She purses her lips. "What other options do we have besides selling the company to Alicia, or Alicia and Adam? I'm not sure I'm comfortable with having our financial future in our kids' hands."

Most of the time, when Aaron introduces this stark reality to parents who are selling their business to their children, they experience fear if not total panic about relinquishing control, placing a huge bet on kids who may not be ready. He expects this will be no different, especially with Ann.

"There's always the option of selling Aardvark to an outsider. John has done a lot to get the company to a point where it's almost sale ready. I'm sure there'd be lots of companies who would love to own Aardvark. In fact, I'd be surprised if John isn't being contacted weekly about outsiders wanting to buy the business."

John confirms that he regularly gets calls about this.

"Although selling to an outside party is a simple solution for your financial independence, it would likely cause some problems with your family."

Ann seems confused, "I don't get it, what sort of problems?"

"Alicia thinks she's been promised the CEO position. If the company is sold to an outsider, chances are good that not only would she not be the CEO, she wouldn't even have a job at the company."

Ann's pain point is Adam. Both men know this. John better understands his wife's near-obsession with their son and her apparent disinterest in Alicia's future, which is why he got straight to the point. "You know, if we sold the company to an outsider, I can promise you that Adam would be fired within the first week of the takeover. His behavior just wouldn't be tolerated by a new owner."

Ann takes the bait and makes a dig or two at John. John lacks patience, she claims, always favoring Alicia over Adam. "I'm so tired of Alicia this and Alicia that, and all the while, Adam is being left by the wayside." She compares John to Aaron's father, having just heard the story.

Aaron knows there is a time to insert Adam into the conversation, and it isn't now. "The most important thing for us to do is to maintain flexibility as far as the financial part of your retirement goes. Since John has no intention of retiring before four and a half years from now, we have time to decide what door we go through. We need to start prepping all involved with what has to happen with the company for both of you to feel comfortable about keeping the business in the family. We've started doing that, and I'm referring to the managers' meeting we held today. But that's just the start."

Ann stops frowning. She leans forward. John grabs a piece of bread and attacks it with butter. The restaurant is filling up now. The soft buzz of conversation can now be heard.

Aaron continues. "Prepping includes having several conversations with Alicia and potentially Adam about what they're going to have to do. We'll need to introduce them to the covenants and agreements that will have to be in place before you're willing to sell them the company. They'll need to understand their importance and the impact those agreements will have on their life. I also recommend we have a conversation with the management team, letting them know your intentions. We discussed the broad strokes today, but they'll be looking for solid decisions on your part, not just possibilities. We also want to let the team know what you'll need to keep the business private. Let's be clear. Keeping the company in the family is in their best interest. They're clear on that front, from what I could tell."

John says, "Can't we wait a couple of years to bring the managers in?"

Aaron answers, "Your managers are wondering what the actual transfer strategy is going to be. They need to know that their performance is one of the major influencers in your decision about how to transfer the business. Your managers' performance will help you decide whether to sell the business to an outsider or to your children. And, the managers will have a major impact on the performance of Aardvark. If they don't significantly improve it, you financially wouldn't be able to afford to keep the business in your family.

"You need to be very clear with everyone, meaning your children and your managers, about what has to happen before you can agree to keep the business in your family."

John realizes that what Aaron is saying is true. He's had several conversations with different managers over the past three months when questions about the company's future would pop up. He'd been ducking the issue. "OK, so I have the conversation with the managers. How do I do this? I have no idea how to present all of this in a positive way. I don't want them bolting."

"Before we have this meeting," Aaron continued, "we need to have a conversation with Alicia about what she needs to do, and we need to decide what the next step is in order for her to take over the business. I think she's mastered her marketing role to the point where she's ready for a new challenge."

The waiter arrives with their dinners. While he sets the food down, the conversation turns to small talk. While they eat, Ann brightens up and tells Aaron about their scheduled trip to Italy.

As they finish dinner, Aaron switches the conversation to his thoughts on Adam. His gut tells him that if he gets John on board with Adam having his own small company, the young man would be successful and experience a nice personality change. "There is lots of work to do over the next four and a half years to get Aardvark where it needs to be. We also have a giant elephant in the room. That elephant is your son."

As soon as Aaron says that, Ann glares at him. "My son is not an elephant; let's be clear." Ann crosses her arms across her chest.

Aaron knows he's on thin ice, yet he continues. "Remember our earlier conversation about the issues I had with my father and how I ended up buying a small part of his company?"

Ann waits without reaction.

"You might also remember I told you that I thought there were similarities between Adam and myself. That's where this crazy idea comes from."

Both Ann and John look at each other, then lean in.

"I think the best way to help your son is to help him own his own small company at least two hours away from Aardvark."

John immediately pushed back from the table and throws his hands up.

"What, you're saying that Adam has the capacity to manage people?" John says. "Have you seen him interact with my team? He's a disaster."

Aaron spends five minutes telling Ann and John why he thinks this is a good idea and how it could solve multiple problems at the same time. Aaron loves when this happens, and it shows on his face.

John leans back in his chair. He is sure this is a harebrained idea. Adam shows no interest in having his own business nor does he show any interest in learning anything about the business besides his little niche in fixing his machines.

At the same time, Adam continues to be a huge problem. John knows at some point he will have to stop protecting him. He wants to know more.

Before he can ask for more information, the waiter reappears and asks if they want dessert. All three decide to share a piece of chocolate cake.

"I'm not sure how Adam would ever be able to run his own company," John said after the waiter leaves. "He's never shown any interest in the general operations, and even a small company is past his ability."

Ann gives John a sharp look. "How do you know? You've never given him the chance."

John ignores his wife. "I have to say, I am a little interested in why you think this could work."

Aaron straightened up in his chair. "I know that my father would have said the same thing about me had the idea been proposed to him in the beginning. He would have said that I didn't know anything about the business." Aaron laughs. "He would have said that but with more intensity, if you catch my drift. In fact, he would have dismissed the idea out of hand." Aaron remembers his father's anger, the disappointment he had caused him. Then he shakes off the sadness. "I was lucky; I forced his hand by picking up the new accounts while I was at the other location.

"I think Adam will benefit for two reasons. One, he'd get away from you," Aaron nods toward John, "and second, he knows he's a problem but doesn't know how to stop being one."

Ann sighs. She studies her hands.

"There's always the possibility we can work with Adam and help him fit in at Aardvark. But that's a really hard thing to do. The second is to let him have a clean start. Although $100,000 is real money, and that's money coming out of Aardvark, it's not that much if things don't work out."

John immediately bolts upright. He can't believe his ears. "You're saying I should fund this shop of his, when he can't behave like a human being? When we're talking about putting enough money aside so we can afford to retire?" Ann pulls at his arm. John ignores her and glares at Aaron.

"You wouldn't be giving him the money. You would co-sign a note that he'd be responsible for."

John can feel his anger rise. He's sick of others covering for his no-good son. "Maybe you were right to tell us your story. Maybe you're seeing something that just isn't there. You're not Adam. You don't know him."

"I think you really underestimate him," Aaron says. "On top of all of this, I sent up a trial balloon. When I talked with him, he seemed to like the idea. I think it's worth a conversation with him about this."

"He liked the idea?" Ann asks.

"It's also a great way to protect him from whatever happens at Aardvark. You're already paying him more than what his replacement would cost. Even at this level, there's no way for him to have the lifestyle both of you have. If he ran his own operation, he'd have a much better chance of having the financial security that I bet both of you want for him."

As Aaron continues talking, he sees Ann relax. She finally smiles. "What do you think?" he asks her.

She looks at her husband, then back at Aaron. "It's a possibility. Going down that road might be worthwhile. Do you really think Adam could make a good living running his own shop?"

"Yes, especially if Aardvark made him one of their vendors. Now, he'd have to understand that acting out would not be acceptable, and you might have to pull some business to prove your point. I'm sure that with any other customers he landed, he wouldn't act that way. Notice that when a customer visits Aardvark, he's a totally different person.

"As to whether he could make a good living, I've seen lots of these shops over the years. You'd be surprised how many of them make $300,000 to $500,000 with just five or ten employees. If run properly, they can be very profitable, just not very salable."

John slips into deep thought. He always thought that had he not started Aardvark, running a machine shop might not have been a bad thing to do. He knows it's something they should at least consider. It could be a solution to many issues.

The three of them agree to consider the Adam option and to meet with Alicia the first thing in the morning for the next step in the transitioning process.

CHAPTER 13

Will Alicia Take Over Aardvark?

●　●　●

The next morning, Ann and John arrive together. They're a little early, and both are nervous about this morning's meeting with Alicia. John knows that Aaron, who will be leading the conversation, tends to be very blunt and upfront. He thinks it's probably best that Aaron is that way for this particular meeting.

Ann and John stayed up late after coming home from dinner. They spent a long time talking about how they'd treated their children differently while they were growing up and even after they'd become young adults. John admitted that he was harder on Adam than Alicia. In his defense, he kept saying that Alicia was easy and Adam wasn't.

Ann didn't disagree with his analysis. She also kept coming back to her point: It really didn't matter that Adam was more difficult than Alicia. They both were their children, and both should have the same amount of love shown them. She felt the need to overcompensate for Adam as a way to protect him from John. Ann went on to say that maybe Aaron's idea would be a way to make it up to Adam.

Before they went to sleep, they'd both come to the same conclusion: It would likely be best for Adam if he got a clean start. They also were willing to see what Aaron proposed when it came to the transfer of the business. They were pretty sure they didn't want their children to be partners. They both realized having a partnership with their children would be a recipe for disaster because they both throw rocks at each other, and they see no reason that would stop. Adam has been allowed to have an attitude at Aardvark while John is running it. Neither thought this would work well if, and when, Alicia took over.

Ann and John are lost in their thoughts while waiting for Aaron and Alicia to arrive.

Aaron comes in through the open door. "Good morning, how did you folks sleep last night?" From his vantage point, both look tired.

"Ann and I had a long conversation about the things we covered at dinner," John says once Aaron takes a seat. "I think we're both in agreement that we want to try to do an internal sale. We know there's risk involved, and we're willing to take it as long as there are several guardrails put up, so if things go wrong, we have a way of protecting ourselves. We think Alicia needs to be aware and, hopefully, a little scared of what she's going to have to promise."

Ann kicks in. "We also think we'd like to have the business owned by Alicia. The problem is we want to make sure we treat both our children equally and fairly. This is not negotiable. If we can't find a way for this to happen, then, in my opinion, there is no way we can let Alicia buy the business by herself."

Right after Ann finishes her thoughts, Alicia walks in. "Sorry, I'm a little late. Had a marketing piece that had to go out this morning and I needed to make sure it was done. The last thing I want to do is think about it during our meeting." She plops into a chair across from her parents.

Aaron admires her confidence. She'll need even more of that when or if she takes over the business. "Let's get started. Your mother, father, and I went out for a long dinner last night. The main topic of conversation revolved around their desire to have the business transferred to you, and if you're up for the job or not."

Alicia flinches. Aaron can see that the word "if" has had a significant effect on her body language. "Your parents would like you to be the next owner of Aardvark. That may come as good news for you, but along with that comes some challenges. I think it's best for all of us to lay our cards on the table and see if we have a clear understanding of what's involved. Does that make sense to you?"

Alicia slowly nods. Her parents watch her intently.

"Let's start with some of the issues that need to be addressed. Please make sure you jump in with any questions you might have.

"I want to start with some observations about the risk your parents are taking."

Alicia bristles. "Risks, what risks?"

"Remember in our managers meeting yesterday we talked about the need for your parents to be financially independent?"

"Of course. We agreed that my parents hadn't put away enough for retirement outside the business. That the sale of the business or whatever we do would have to provide a pretty big part of the money they need for retirement." She doesn't sound defensive to Aaron, just matter of fact.

John and Ann remain quiet. John doesn't want to say anything until Aaron finishes his line of questioning. He thinks Alicia sounds defensive and wants to jump in. For the time being, he decides to be quiet.

Aaron nods. "That's the biggest risk they face. What happens if you take over the business and then it flounders? Or even worse, ends up being insolvent? Or, what happens if you take over the company, and they realize you don't have what it takes to run the company? Both are big risks we need to do our best to manage."

Alicia looks at both her parents and picks at her sweater. "I'm confused. Why am I the one who has to shoulder all the risks?"

John starts to speak, and Aaron holds up his hand for John not to say anything.

Alicia's reaction is what he expects. It's time for the "come to Papa" conversation. It's time for Alicia to hear what many parents worry about when they turn the business over to their children. He also knows that John is getting hot under the collar. He suspects John is upset that Alicia doesn't understand where he and his wife are coming from.

"The reason you have to be responsible for these risks is, first, you're going to be the next owner of Aardvark. Second, you're young. If you screw it up, you have plenty of time to recover. Your parents don't. If you screw it up, there goes their retirement. Third, you've done a great job in marketing, but you've yet to be tested. Running a company is an entirely different ball of wax. In fact, we need to talk about what your next job here will be during this meeting."

Alicia seems to take the reasons under consideration. She loses her defensive stance. "OK, I get that there are risks with them selling me the company. But I'd never allow the company or them to suffer because of my bad decisions." She looks at her parents. "You believe that, don't you?"

Ann jumps in. "Honey, we know you'd never purposefully hurt either of us. But, things happen. None of us can see that far down the road. If any of those things happen, you might not know what to do. You could, not for lack of trying, make a decision that would hurt the company. Maybe to the point where the company couldn't recover. That's what we need to protect ourselves from."

John adds, "Your mother has named our issue. We think that, in time, you'll be ready and will do a great job. On the other hand, I've had too many friends who've had their businesses blow up after they transitioned to new owners. In two cases, they ended up losing everything."

Aaron is impressed. "That's exactly what we're talking about. Since your mom brought that up first, let's start there.

"As long as you run the company in a financially responsible manner, neither your mother nor father will interfere with what you're doing. What we want is for you to understand that your parents are playing bank for you. Since they're going to be a bank, they need to act like a bank. That means that when you buy the company, you're going to have what's called loan covenants."

"Loan covenants?" Alicia raises an eyebrow.

Aaron explains the concept.

"An example would be a debt to equity ratio, which means you'll need to hold a ratio where the amount of debt the company has is no more than what the amount of equity there is in the company. There are plenty more that we'll develop, and just remember, your parents are your bank, and they need to act like a bank."

Aaron notes Alicia's frown. She needs to learn this stuff. Aaron is a little curious as to why Alicia doesn't know about basic financial ratios. He assumed she would have learned about them in her MBA finance courses. "There are several things you'll be required to do to make sure he doesn't have that right, and maintaining the correct financial ratios is just one of them."

"Like what?"

Aaron has this conversation with all junior family members who are taking over a business. He wants to provide just enough information for Alicia to wake up to what will happen if she screws up. Over the next four and a half years, other factors will be revealed as everyone thinks about the protections her parents need. All of it doesn't need to be discussed at this moment.

"Let's start with your dashboard. This is where we summarize important information your father will need to monitor the company. We're going to have to beef up the information you provide your father on a weekly and monthly basis. Some of the things he'll be monitoring include cash in bank, your financial ratios, receivables, payables, new sales, and backlog. There might be more than these. But these measurement are a start.

"It really comes down to what are the rules of the road. This means when can your father have a legal right to step in and run the company and when he can't. The more definitive we can be about this, the less chance we'll have a major disagreement down the road. I'm hoping you'll ask your father for advice. A big mistake I often see is the junior generation forgets the wisdom and knowledge the senior generation has, even years after they've sold the business."

Alicia looks horrified. "You mean if I have a bad month, I'll lose control of the company?" She folds her arms across her chest.

John is getting the reaction he wants. He likes the idea of Aaron playing the heavy. As much as John ends up being the bad guy, he doesn't enjoy it.

"Not necessarily. The covenants will allow your father to take over the board if you're out of trust, meaning you failed to live up to one or more of the agreed upon covenants. I've worked with a lot of other companies. When the company has floundered, and it's happened often enough, both the senior and junior members of the family worked together to solve the problem. It doesn't get fixed any other way."

John finally pipes in. "Look, sweetheart. I have no interest in taking back the company once you take over. Mom and I do, however, have an interest in making sure we get paid. And the only way that happens is if the business prospers. I have tons of confidence that you'll do fine. These safeguards are actually for both our protection." Alicia turns her face away, stares at the wall. John continues, "I know you might not think so right now. That makes perfect sense to me." Ann reaches her hand out and pats John's knee.

Aaron feels the tension rising in the room. He knows the next topic he has to bring up will raise it even more. "There is one more thing we need to talk about on this subject before we move on. There's something getting in the way of us having an open and honest conversation."

All eyes turn to Aaron.

John speaks up first, "I think the conversation is going quite well." He doesn't notice that Alicia is seething.

Aaron presses forward. "OK. Let's talk about the unspoken issue. It appears to me that there's a lack of trust here." He turns his gaze on Alicia. "On your parents' part, the issue is how competent you are now and how competent you will be when you take over the company." Alicia turns her nose up. "I'm going to bet that you feel as though your parents don't really care about you even though, in your rational mind, you know they do." She shrugs, and Aaron isn't sure he's getting through.

Aaron thinks it's a good time to review the trust formula. He'd spoken about it the last time he worked with Aardvark. A review won't hurt. "When I start to see tempers rise, I almost always know there's an issue with trust that we need to deal with. I found this formula years ago in a book called *The Trusted Advisor*." He reaches for a marker and goes to the whiteboard in John's office and writes:

Credibility + Intimacy + Reliability / Self-Interest

They all look at the formula he's written on the board.

"That formula will tell you how much or how little you trust others and how others trust you. In the conversation we're having now, Alicia is having a problem with intimacy, which affects her sense of security when interacting with you. This leads her to question how much you care about her." He nods at John and Ann. "You have a credibility issue, which often translates to competence, meaning you question how well Alicia can run the company." He drops the marker on the whiteboard ledge. "And that's what's causing the temperature to rise in the room right now."

John makes a mental note to remind Aaron to bring this formula up again when they talk with Adam. Then he turns to his daughter. "If we're going to get you ready to take over the company, I need to know what the next step is for you. You're doing a great job with marketing, and I think it's time for you to take on some more responsibility." Alicia opens her mouth but hesitates. John continues, "I don't expect you to know. Aaron, do you have any ideas?"

"As it happens, I do." He waits a beat to make sure it's okay with Alicia that he offers an opinion on her trajectory. "There's a role in large companies that often exists, and I've seen that role become more common in smaller ones. I think this role will be a terrific training ground for Alicia and also make sense for Aardvark. So, the next step for Alicia is to become the chief revenue officer of the company."

None of the others seem to recognize the title.

"A CRO is the person responsible for all parts of a company in which revenue is produced or influenced. Typically, and I suggest this for Aardvark, that person is responsible for sales, marketing, customer service, and outside innovation. Those are the four areas of the company that influence revenue in a direct manner."

John considers the concept for a moment. He likes the idea. He knows Alicia is ready for the next step. He also thinks that announcing this new role for Alicia might bring the temperature down. His management team has been looking for a move on his part so they can gauge their future, Alicia is gunning for more responsibility, and this role is a natural next step. John needs to know that he'll eventually be able to walk away, even if the thought scares him in other ways. Over the next year or so, he'll get a sense for whether Alicia really will be up for taking over the company with this new role. Or not.

Aaron watches Alicia intently as he further explains this new role. He sees her breathing return to normal and her shoulders become less hunched. When he decides that she's on board for the moment, he turns his attention back to John and Ann.

"John, what do you think about the idea of having a CRO, having Alicia take on the role?"

"Makes sense." He considers the possible benefits. "Those parts of the company don't communicate very well anyway. Having Alicia responsible for everything that creates revenue could do two things. It might stop the infighting between them. And we'll get to see how well she can learn to delegate." He looks at his daughter, who is clearly paying attention. Unlike Adam, she can be angry, but she'll also listen. "In her present marketing role, it's just her and an assistant. She doesn't really have to delegate at all. Taking this on would force her to work through others. I know that last time you were here this was a really hard lesson for me to learn. I suspect the same will be true for Alicia."

Aaron turns to Alicia. "What do you think?"

"I like the idea. To tell you the truth, I've been starting to get a little bored with what I'm doing now. We've got marketing running pretty smoothly, and there's not a lot of challenge for me anymore. I'd love to work with Stan on sales. And I think our innovation process could use some work." She turns to her father. "Right now, it's all about you, Dad. When you leave, I'm not sure… who will take over. I know that sounds silly because we're all sitting around here talking about me taking over. But when it comes to innovation, I'm going to need a lot of help from someone. I don't know; I think I'm going to need help in that area from you."

Aaron is getting ready to bring the meeting to a close. Before he can talk, John jumps in. "I was worried there for a while," he says to Alicia, "that you just want to kick me out and take over as fast as you can."

Aaron says, "I think we're well on our way. I know four and a half years sounds like a long way out, but I can tell you, it'll be here way before we're totally ready. Starting to lay the groundwork now for what's going to happen a few years out is just good planning. It's the responsible thing to do.

"Just remember that when things get tough, and they will, look to the trust formula to figure out what you need to do to fix any tension in the room. I can tell you it's a tool I use almost every day, especially when I see communication breaking down."

Aaron gets up and stretches. A cup of coffee is in his future, and he wants to get a little caffeine in him before the next meeting with Adam. He suspects this one will be a lot tougher for all three of them than the one they've just finished with Alicia.

CHAPTER 14

Adam Makes a Decision

● ● ●

Ann is holding one of John's toys from his desk when the two men come back. "You guys were gone for a while. What's up?"

John shrugs and looks at Aaron.

"We had a short conversation about some of the challenges that John would personally have with Alicia taking more responsibility here. I'm sure we'll be having that conversation more than once."

With that, Adam saunters in and closes the door behind him.

Aaron is astounded. This is the first time he's seen Adam enter a room without causing a full-on explosion. He hopes Adam's entry bodes well for the conversation they're about to have.

Everyone takes a seat. Adam and his mother sit on the couch, and John and Aaron take their usual seats. Everyone looks at Aaron. Aaron gets it. He's not only a business mentor and thinking partner; he sometimes ends up playing therapist as well. Aaron knows his abilities in this area are limited, so he has strict guidelines that he follows. If he feels the conversation is getting into an area that requires a higher level of help than he's willing or able to give, he has several business therapists he brings in. He isn't expecting that to happen today, but with Adam, he never knows. "I guess it's up to me to start the conversation." Looking at Adam, he adds, "If there's anything I get wrong from our conversation yesterday, please speak up."

Adam gives him a thumbs up, smirks.

"OK, let's get started. I had this thought that I ran by Adam yesterday. I recognized some similarities between the way I grew up with my father and the way Adam has grown up." Aaron notices Adam visibly relax. "I managed to get a business up and running away from him, and I think my father was surprised at how much I knew about business. I think the same may hold true for Adam."

John wonders what Aaron's been smoking but decides to stay quiet and see where this all leads.

Aaron continues, "He's grown up with you two talking about business for years." Aaron directs his hand first toward John and then to Ann." He's heard the stories, good and bad. Now, Adam hasn't had the advantage of working for someone else. That's not totally unusual in the world of family business. It's not optimal, yet it happens all of the time." Aaron reiterates the plan for Adam to purchase a machine shop and his faith that Adam has the ability to run it.

Adam appears perfectly relaxed. Aaron knows, having spoken with Adam briefly, that Adam has thought about the idea and agrees that it would be a good thing for him to do.

Everyone looks at each other. Aaron wonders who will speak first. He doesn't have to wait long.

John goes first. "OK, assuming that Adam has the skills he needs, beyond the tech skills, which I know he has, how is he going to afford to buy a company?" He goes on to express his concerns about finding a replacement for his son.

Aaron expected this question. "Let's talk about replacing him here first. You likely won't have to pay his replacement more money because you're paying Adam more than what someone else would cost. Sure, it'll be a bit inconvenient, but between George and Janice, they'll be able to figure it out."

Adam clearly can't contain himself. "George! He's a total waste of time. The dude has got to go."

John wants to throttle Adam. "We're not talking about George. And frankly, I could care less about your opinion."

Aaron intervenes. "Look, we need both of you to stop triggering each other if we're ever going to get anywhere. One more reason why the two of you can't work together. Don't you get tired of this sniping?"

Ann fidgets in her chair. "Every time I'm in the same room with you two, I want to scream. Is there any way you could try to be civil with each other? You have no idea how uncomfortable it makes everyone around you. I know neither of you care, but I do, and I'm sick of it."

Neither Adam nor John take responsibility for the outburst. Aaron is too easily triggered by his son, and Adam seems to delight in poking his father. Aaron's no psychologist, but if Adam remains at the company, they'd both need therapy. All the more reason Adam needs to leave the company.

"Let's move on to how Adam could afford to buy a small machine tooling company. John, you would co-sign the note, and Adam, you'd be responsible for paying the bank back. I've seen this done many times. Families that are worth hundreds of millions of dollars call this setup the family bank." Once again, Aaron focuses his attention on John, then Ann. "You're not in a position to put together a family bank. But, John, you do have the ability to co-sign the note. Adam would be committing to all of the guarantees, so you wouldn't have to step in unless Adam defaulted on the note. If he did, you could absorb the loss if you absolutely had to."

Ann speaks up. "My vote is we put Adam into his own business. It might be the only way we'll ever have a civil conversation in our family. At some point, I would like to see us have a Thanksgiving dinner that didn't include full-on shouting."

Aaron sees that the decision has been made, and Ann is the one who's made it. He often sees this sort of resolution when dealing with a tough family issue. Mom steps in and makes a declaration, and everyone else agrees.

Adam isn't done with his nonsense. "OK, I get to have my own little crappy company. I actually like that idea. But what about Aardvark? You're going to give Alicia the whole company, which is worth millions. All you're doing is setting me up with a token that'll cost you $100,000. Actually, I'll be the one paying for it anyway. Pardon me." Adam turns to his mother. "Like that's fair."

John looks to Aaron for help on this one. Deep down, he fears that Adam is right. What would that mean about him? How the family wealth should be handled needs to be dealt with now. Although he and Ann talked with Aaron about this yesterday, he bets that Ann probably doesn't remember the details. One look at her and John knows she's about to pick up their son's cause and run him through with it like a sword. He turns to Aaron. "Would you be willing to explain to my genius son what our plans are? I know I could use a refresher, and I bet Ann could use one also."

"Sure. If you remember, Alicia would be allowed to buy the company after proving she can run the whole thing. She'd pay a fair market price for the business. We'd have to get a business valuation, and that would be the number she'd pay." Aaron turns to Adam. "So, you see, Alicia will be paying for her business too." He resumes, making it clear that he's talking to Ann and John. "We'll do our best to make sure that we do the transaction in a tax-friendly way for Alicia. She's the one who has the biggest tax cost if we do a stock sale."

John and Ann both look confused. John says, "Why is the stock sale more expensive taxwise?"

Aaron answers, "Stock is always bought with after-tax dollars. Most of the time, we don't think about this. For example, let's say I'm going to buy your business for $1,000,000. If I'm in the 40% tax bracket, the real cost is $1,800,000. That's because before I can pay you the $1,000,000 for the business, I have to earn enough money to pay the taxes and then give the rest to you.

"We'll be working on methods to reduce the tax cost, and I don't want to get into that right now. Let's stay on the estate stuff so Adam knows what we're thinking." He turns to Ann and John. "The money that's paid for the business would come to both of you, and it would be part of your estate. After both of you die, the estate would be split 50/50 between Alicia and Adam. Most people find this to be the fairest way to split an estate."

Aaron then looks at Adam. "What do you think of that idea?"

"Well, it sounds OK, I guess. I'm sure that somehow I'll get screwed. I always get screwed, particularly when it comes to Alicia."

John feels himself getting hot again and really wants to pick a fight with Adam. He remembers what Aaron told him when this happens. He takes a deep breath and lets the moment pass.

Aaron decides to ignore the comment. "I guess we've come to a conclusion of sorts. We've agreed. Adam will leave the company. John and Adam will try to work together to find an appropriate small machine shop to buy that's at least two hours away from here. Alicia will continue to be groomed to take over the business. In about four and a half years, she'll buy the company from John. She'll sign a bunch of agreements that allow John to step back in if she doesn't do a great job."

Ann leans back against the couch. Adam relaxes as well. John nods each time Aaron ticks off an item that they've covered during the meeting.

"Alicia will pay the fair market price for the business. John and Ann will use the money for their retirement, and after they're gone, the estate will be split 50/50 between Adam and Alicia. Adam will have no direct financial interest in Aardvark, and Alicia will have no direct financial interest in the machine shop he owns.

"Does that sound about right to everyone?"

For the first time in the meeting, Ann smiles. "This works. I just hope these decisions will help bring our family a little closer." She reaches for Adam and lays a hand by his leg. "I just get so tired and worn out with the arguing."

Adam slowly nods. "I guess it sounds OK to me. At least I'll get away from this jerk." He flicks his thumb toward his father. His sounds typically glum, not angry.

"Let's call this the working plan," says Aaron with an air of finality.

CHAPTER 15

Janice's Future at Aardvark

⬡ ⬡ ⬡

Aaron finds his way to the conference room where Janice is already waiting. He nods at Janice and gets a cup of coffee, sits down with a big sigh. He's tired. It's not often he has to deal with someone like Adam. If that were the entire engagement, he would have withdrawn long ago.

John then enters with Alicia. As usual, John sits at the head of the table with the two women on either side of him.

"Why don't you start off with a recap of where we are now?" Aaron asks John, despite knowing that John prefers to let him run these meetings so he can watch everyone's reactions.

John's confused. "A full recap? Or just the parts that are relevant to the group?"

Aaron offers him a mischievous smile. "I'll let you decide."

John has to spend a few seconds gathering his thoughts. He wonders if he should go into the Adam decision or just focus on the Janice-related stuff. He really hates airing his dirty laundry. What if the people on the management team, Janice in particular, think he's getting soft or weak? He doesn't like that idea at all. He isn't sure what he wants to do. Eventually, he decides the whole conversation would make more sense if he just came out with it all.

John starts, "There are four main things we need to talk about in this meeting. The role of Janice moving forward, Alicia's path toward becoming our next CEO, Adam's future, and, of course, Aardvark finances, what we'll need from the company for all of this to work."

Aaron's impressed. He expected John to leave out the part about Adam and to skim past the financial needs. "That's a good agenda for the time we have together. Where shall we start?"

John knows Janice likes to have all of the available details. She shuts down when he doesn't share the whole story, and she seems to always sense when he's holding back. Over the past several years, she and John have developed a deep level of trust. Now it's time to test that trust.

Janice pipes up. "I'm really curious about Adam."

Aaron fills her in on Adam and his plans.

"I thought he'd be here forever," Janice says when he's finished.

Aaron smiles. She's always struck him as a pragmatic woman who likes consistency. She may not like Adam, but she seems truly surprised by the announcement. Aaron says, "I did too, that was until our conversation with him.

"As a side note, I believe there's a good chance you'll see a big change in Adam over the next few years. I find it curious that when second generations are allowed to do their own thing, they often blossom in ways no one would ever expect."

Alicia looks at the paper in front of her and clears her throat.

Aaron continues, "Let's move on from Adam. We'll have to have George work on replacing him. Mind you, I don't think George will see that as an unpleasant activity."

Janice stifles a laugh.

"Let's tackle the hard part next. Let's talk about John and Ann's financial needs and how they relate to the work we do here." He goes on to review what they've all determined thus far.

Aaron nods at Janice first, then Alicia. "You both understand the financial gap between the sale of the company to Alicia and their retirement savings. If the internal transfer happens in four and a half years, we'll need Aardvark to be more valuable, to have the ability to pay them more for the company. If that doesn't happen, well, John will be forced to sell the company to a third party."

Aaron feels the temperature of the room immediately rise. They've had the conversation before, but the news still upsets both women.

Aaron continues. "Again, whether the company is sold to Alicia or it's sold to an outsider totally depends on the work you do between now and the time John retires. That means you've got time to affect the outcome. I'll bet John will give you a little more time if you need it. That being said, I know that Ann will be watching our progress closely. If it looks like we can't hit the necessary financial metrics, Ann will probably force John to look for an outside buyer."

John is confused. He thought he would be the one to make the decision. Then he remembers a conversation he and Aaron had about spouses always being more concerned about family finances than the business owner. Because of this, Ann will likely be watching the financial progress of Aardvark more closely than John.

"We've already talked with Alicia about what sort of promises she needs to make, and if she wants, she can share them with you later. For the time being, let's just understand we need to improve the financial performance of the company."

"OK," Janice says, "we need to improve the performance of Aardvark. By how much? And what will our milestones be?"

Aaron admires Janice's all-in attitude, but he expects she'll eventually feel some fear. She has a lot at stake. "We're going to need to improve the free cash flow by about $300,000 per year." He doesn't have to look to know that Janice's jaw has dropped. "I know that sounds like a lot, but it's really a 50% improvement, which is a lot, but not so much that the company can't do it. With the team you have, and with you bringing in key players like George, the goal is realistic. You'll have to work hard to get there, but I have every confidence you will."

John pipes up, "When I look back at what we've already accomplished, it seems to me that this is a very doable activity. After all, that's only about a 10% improvement a year, and we've been doing much better than that."

Janice has another question. This time she seems to choose her words carefully. "If Alicia takes over at that point, provided we get to that point, what happens to me?" She reaches for the water glass before her. Takes a sip of water. "Like I said, I'd love it if I could end my working career here and have enough money to retire comfortably. Is that part of the plan?" She doesn't ask Aaron; she asks John.

John jumps in. "We're going to put together a bonus plan for you. If we hit our goals or there's a sale to an outside company, regardless, you'll be taken care of financially. As far as what happens to your role here, I'm going to let Aaron explain."

Aaron studies Alicia while John reassures Janice. He's interested in her reaction. He notices that she's staying calm, which she'll need to do if she's to be successful.

Aaron pulls his attention back to Janice. "In the situation Aardvark is in, where we're going through a generational change, there's always the challenge of getting the junior generation ready to take over the company. In too many companies, the senior generation, the parent, is responsible for that preparation. When this happens, it almost never goes well. For example, all of the family dynamics of growing up get in the way, and as you can see with Adam, that often doesn't work out very well. If instead, like we mean to do here, we have a professional manager supervise the younger generation, the whole transition goes so much smoother. It's a win-win for everyone involved.

"If everything goes well, and I assume everything will, at some point the manager and the junior member of the family switch positions. This means that around the time John retires, you, Janice, will directly report to Alicia instead of her reporting to you. I call this the leapfrog transition.

"This doesn't mean your career ends here when Alicia becomes CEO. It means you'll continue in your role as Integrator/Chief Operating Officer of the company. It also means you've done a great job of getting Alicia ready to take over the company. I see no reason that you won't continue as the senior member of the team and a continued mentor to Alicia."

Janice seems to take it all in. She also appears to have a lot of questions. "OK, I get that part, the COO part. Let's talk about Alicia's new role. What are we going to have her do now? How do we get her trained?"

"Let me start with what problem we're trying to solve first. In most companies, and Aardvark is no exception, there is no one who coordinates all of the revenue-producing activities. I'm recommending we have Alicia take this one with the title of Chief Revenue Officer. This will be a challenging role for Alicia. Not only will she be responsible for the four areas of profit, but she'll also have to learn how to delegate. The delegation part is where your influence will be crucial for Alicia's success. John and I both think this is the next logical step for Alicia to take."

Aaron worries that John will grow impatient while implementing all of the things that will need to be done. He knows the success of the transition is going to lie mostly on Janice's shoulders. He's confident that he and Janice will be able to work together, sometimes even doing an end run around John, to get the company in shape for John and Ann to retire.

Aaron realizes that Alicia has remained quiet. He's curious as to what she makes of the plan and if she's gotten any clarity in the short time she's had to think it over. He asks her for her thoughts. She reiterates what she said in the last meeting, her excitement around bringing unity to customer service, marketing, innovation, and sales.

Aaron likes the answer. John does also. Janice, however, has a question. "Have you folks thought about Stan and what his reaction is going to be? He's had a free hand in sales, and I'm not sure he's going to take kindly to having Alicia manage him. He's used to reporting to John, and it took him a long time to get used to reporting to me. I'm afraid he's going to see this as a demotion of sorts."

"Good point," John says.

Aaron hadn't thought about that potential issue. "You're right. We're going to have to find a good way to let Stan know that we're aware of the changes, what they mean for him and why, ultimately, they'll be good for him. I'm pretty sure he's going to want to still be here after John retires. If we help him realize that reporting to Alicia is his best option, it might help bring him on board. We'll have to hear out Stan's reservations. The best way to do that, in my opinion, is to ask him."

Aaron smiles at everyone. "Let's call it quits for now. I see we have about ninety minutes before our next meeting. This is going to be an important one. We're getting close to making action plans; I want everyone to be excited about the direction we're going. And that means we'll need to have some honest conversations."

CHAPTER 16

A Fully Funded Company

⬡ ⬡ ⬡

John picks Aaron up in the reception area after the lunch break, and they walk back to the conference room together.

"How was your lunch meeting?" Aaron is just a little curious, and the small talk is probably an OK thing. The conversations they've been having are intense, to say the least.

"It was good. I had a lunch thing set up with my attorney, and we talked about our work. He was most interested in the Adam solution and thinks it could work, but he cautioned me about being on the hook for the money."

Aaron makes a mental note to have a conversation with John's attorney about his reservations.

John and Aaron move into the conference room with five minutes to spare before the scheduled start. The entire management team is present. Janice has moved chairs to allow John to take the head. Aaron sits toward the back. Aaron always sits in that position because it's better to lead from the back. John has never understood his reasoning.

John starts. "We've got a lot to cover today. I'm hoping that, by the end of this meeting, we have some agreement and a general direction we'll be heading, at least for the foreseeable future." He gestures to Aaron to carry on.

Aaron observes the body language in the room. Janice and Alicia are open and seemingly ready to get to work. George's eyes dart from person to person as if searching for clues for what's about to occur. Jack and Stan both have their arms crossed. They look as though they're waiting for the other shoe to drop, even though the first shoe has yet to drop. It's time to let them in on what this meeting is about.

"Yesterday, we talked about how having a sustainable business fit in with the steps of transition all of us at Aardvark will be going through, particularly John. We weren't quite sure where John and Ann are regarding their retirement needs. As suspected, we're going to need to improve our financial performance for the company to stay in the family and for John and Ann to be fully funded for retirement.

John rubs the back of his neck. He's glad to have Aaron leading the charge because he's already exhausted.

"There are also some changes that John, Alicia, and Janice have talked about that will affect us all. John, why don't you start the conversation with what we're thinking about doing with Adam."

He shoots Aaron a dirty look. This part he'd like to skip. Instead, he opens his mouth. "We all know Adam can be challenging to work with. But, he's brilliant at keeping our machines running and solving our really difficult machining tasks. I also know that George and Adam have been like oil and water ever since George arrived." He tips his head toward George whose face remains neutral.

"I've wanted to find a solution. But until yesterday," he spreads his hands wide open, "that wasn't happening. After a series of conversations, we've all decided it's best that Adam moves on." John goes on to share the details. He says, "I trust there won't be any financial stress on Aardvark as a result of this change."

George grins, which ticks John off. It's one thing for him to see his son get his due for bad behavior, it's another thing entirely for someone else to enjoy it. "I'm glad you're happy because you've got a real challenge in front of you. We're going to need to find a replacement for Adam. You might think it'll be easy, but I doubt it. Adam is usually the only one who can fix the older machines that break down, and I have zero intention of approving funds to replace them. So, you're going to need to find someone who can do the job."

George kicks in. "I'll do my best. But I've got to say, I'm not sure it's going to be one person. I think we can reassign some people here and there. And we'll probably have to bring in two people from the outside. It's going to cost us a little more money than we're spending right now. But it'll be worth it."

John thinks George needs to do better than try. This is crucial, and if he blows it, there'll be hell to pay. "Put the company at risk, and I'm never going to be able to retire." Irritated, he throws it back to Aaron.

Aaron walks over to the whiteboard, picks up a marker, and starts writing and talking at the same time. "We've already talked about Adam, so we don't need to add that to our agenda. We'll talk about Alicia's new role at the company and how it will affect all of us. We also need to talk about the Aardvark challenges we're going to have with getting John and Ann to financial independence. And finally, we'll talk about the decision points John and Ann will have on whether Alicia will buy the company or if they'll sell to a third party."

Aaron steps back and looks around the room after he adds the last item to the agenda. He decides, based on the surprised and disturbed body language, that the third item needs to be first on the agenda.

"Let's start here," Aaron taps the third-party sale line item. "If we don't, I can't imagine any of you listening or paying attention to the first two items.

"Even though you've possibly not thought about John's options for leaving the business, you likely know that his plan is to sell the business to Alicia. He's been saying for years that he wants to keep the business in the family. What he's never said—and I'm not sure he's really thought about it until yesterday—is what will happen if she either can't run the company or the company can't be turned into a good retirement source for him and Ann."

John catches Stan, George, and Jack eyeing him. He knows what he's about to say next is important. If he doesn't get it right, he will seriously hurt morale and performance at the company.

Aaron continues. "Again, John's first option is to keep the business in the family and sell it to Alicia. His ability to do so will be dependent on two things. First, Alicia's ability to run the company. And to a large degree, that will depend on all of you to help her learn what she needs to know."

Alicia glances around the room, then trains her eyes on the blackboard.

"I think she's up for that and hope you are too. Second, we need to make sure the company is successful enough financially to afford to buy John's shares at a price that will provide enough cash for a comfortable retirement for Ann and John."

Stan rolls his shoulders forward and crosses his arms. Jack slumps even further into his chair than he normally does. Neither looks happy.

Aaron looks directly at Jack and Stan. "Let's be realistic here. We always need to have a plan B. In this case, plan B is selling to an outside party. If we hit the benchmarks that we establish, plan B won't be an issue. If we don't, then we need to take a look in the mirror and take responsibility for what happens next. It really comes down to what we can accomplish as a team to make the financial part of the plan work."

Jack sits up. "If you ask me. I think we'll need to be far more disciplined in how we spend money around here. We've been on a spending spree. I bet we can find ways of dialing that stuff back and creating some excess cash."

Stan pipes up too. "I guess showing some more discipline in our sales process would also help. That's something I can do."

Aaron doesn't want to get into the weeds at this meeting. He wants to keep the conversation at a higher level. He knows the team members are afraid, that they're scrambling for immediate solutions to assuage their fears, but he wants them to focus on the big picture. "I know that with the stakes being what they are, you'll all come up with great ideas we can put in place. It's just not the right time now to get into the weeds.

"Let's move to our next item." Aaron walks back to the whiteboard and crosses off John's retirement options and circles Alicia's new role.

"This is where we're going to need everyone's help. Alicia is going to have a new role and we need to spend some time discussing it. She'll be adding three areas to her responsibility. Her title will be Chief Revenue Officer." He explains the role for those who hadn't heard about it before. "This means she'll be responsible for marketing. and she'll also be responsible for sales, external product innovation, and customer service."

Aaron makes sure to look at Stan while he speaks. As he suspects, Stan visibly winces at the announcement. Aaron knows that Stan and John have worked closely for years. He knows it's important for John to speak directly to Stan.

John and Aaron exchange a look of understanding. John nods. John knows he will have a private conversation with Stan right after the meeting. He's worked with Stan long enough to know that he's a worrywart. He'll reassure Stan and let him know he's valued and that John wants to make sure Stan's input is listened to.

Aaron continues. "The first thing Alicia is going to need to do is learn from those who are already running a section. The big lesson she'll have to learn is how to be an effective delegator. None of us, and especially Alicia, want to upset the apple cart. Things are going pretty well here. I'm sure she'll want to make some changes, and that would be natural when we start having the four parts of the company that make up revenue activities communicating with each other more effectively. Again, I want to emphasize that the first thing she'll be doing is learning from those who are already in those positions."

Alicia maintains a neutral expression, but Aaron realizes that such a change in responsibility has to carry with it some major anxiety. Stan, on the other hand, seems to exhale and start breathing again.

John has worked with Stan for so long that he can read his most subtle mood changes. He likes what Aaron has to say and wants to add his thoughts. "My first choice is to have Alicia take over the company and buy it from me. That's not a secret. We all agree here. That means she needs to learn a lot more about the business before she does so. I'm really proud of the team we've built here and know that she has an opportunity I never had."

Stan gives him a quizzical look.

"Alicia gets to start with a company that runs pretty well and is profitable. She won't have to go through those beginning days when Stan and I did all of the sales. Remember, Stan? Most of that was like banging our heads against the wall." Stan laughs. "Aardvark has a great reputation, and it's not a big problem to get in front of the type of customers we want to serve. That makes life a lot easier. We're talking a world of difference from when we first started."

Stan smiles. "Yeah, those were the bad old days. It wasn't much fun getting doors slammed in our face." He leans back in his chair. "I will say one thing, life has gotten easier now that we have a good marketing program." He nods appreciatively at Alicia. "I'm curious to see how things will change when we put all four of those areas under one person."

Time is running short. Aaron wants to get to one more thing before the meeting is adjourned.

"Alicia's big challenge will be to manage competing needs and wants. For years, all those areas operated pretty independently of each other. Now we're going to do our best to coordinate the efforts of all four. I suspect that six months from now, you're going to find that our financial goals will start to be realized because of the integration.

"This will require that we find a way to work together and not against each other. I've seen a little sniping from each area, and one of the things I love about a Chief Revenue Officer is it gives all the revenue functions a chance to work as one team. That's our goal, and I'm hopeful we'll get there sooner than anyone in the room thinks."

Aaron needs to wrap up the meeting. It's getting late in the day, and there are a couple more conversations he needs to have before he leaves tomorrow morning.

"If we can, let's call it quits for now. I'll be back here next week, and we'll start working on what we want to accomplish over the next twelve weeks. In the meantime, thanks so much for your time. I really appreciate it."

Aaron and John get up to leave. It's time for Aaron to wrap up the work they've done with Ann and John.

CHAPTER 17

What's Next for John?

● ● ●

A fter the managers meeting, John and Aaron go back to his office where they're due to meet Ann. Before he leaves, Aaron wants to have a final review of what they've covered, what they've agreed to, and what plans need to be put in place over the next three months. A three-month timeframe will allow John and his team to focus on one or two projects. Longer time frames usually involve too many projects, which all fall behind because of the lack of focus. One thing at a time is the way to go.

Aaron knows that John loves his annual budgets. He also knows that most of the time those budgets need to be revised at least two or three times during the year. He doesn't want Aardvark to stop doing those annual budgets. He just wants to make sure that John and Jack spend more time focusing on a rolling three-month time horizon than one for a year, meaning they're always looking out three months and back three months. Aaron also wants to make sure John and Jack start including Janice and Alicia in these conversations. It's time for John to start stepping back, even though he doesn't plan to leave the company for four and a half years.

Speaking of John's exit, John will need to put a closing date on the calendar. This gives everyone a solid date they need to be shooting for, particularly Alicia.

Ann is waiting for them when they get back to the office. She's fiddling with the toys on John's desk again. They all take their usual seats.

Squishy ball in hand, Ann starts. "Where are we with all of the things we talked about? What did you say about Adam?"

John looks at Aaron in the hopes that he'll field Ann's questions.

Aaron is happy to step in. "Let's start with Adam. John announced that Adam would be leaving the company, that he'd be buying his own machine shop. We didn't offer a time frame, but I think we left it that it would happen as soon as we could work things out."

Ann smiles. "So, you've made a public commitment. How'd it go over?"

John answers. "You'd be surprised. No one was doing a happy dance, even George. Everyone realized that there's going to be a big hole created that'll need to be filled.

And filling it will be more difficult than they may have thought."

Ann smiles at this news.

"We also talked about our needs, that if we don't get them met, we won't be able to sell the business to Alicia. We announced that Alicia would be taking a new role on, Chief Revenue Officer of the company."

Ann asks, "How'd that go over?"

John continues. "I don't think anyone was surprised by the promotion. At first, no one really understood what a CRO is, so Aaron had to explain it. I think Stan was a little put off, but he'll be fine. He'll just have to process it. Stan never does change especially well. Alicia will learn she has to move slowly with him."

Aaron doesn't have much time left and wants to make sure he covers a few things with Ann and John before he leaves. "We need to talk about your financial planning as well as some things I want you two to plan for separately and apart."

Ann and John exchange glances. John leans against the arm of the chair and puts his chin in his hand. Ann sits back and waits.

Aaron reviews why the financial plan is important and tells them it needs to be done in the next three months. He reminds John that he's already talked about using the financial planner who does his 401(k) plan.

"Remember, and this is important, don't let the planner you work with reduce how much money you'll spend in retirement. That might happen, and then again, it might not. In the first few years of retirement, you'll usually spend more money and then it'll level off or drop in your later years, provided you don't experience any major health issues. I find it easier to just keep your spending where it is and let it average out in the long run."

John says, "OK, I got that. I'll call our planner this afternoon. He's been asking, and I've been resisting. What's next?"

"Ann, this might be a tough one for you; I know it's going to be a tough one for John." Ann raises a curious eyebrow. "We need to start giving John a taste of life post-Aardvark. Sometime in the next six months, I want John to leave Aardvark for two weeks. No calling in; no coming into the office. John, you and I have talked about this before, at least in general terms. We need to bring Ann into the plan now."

Ann says, "That'll be easy. He can't come to the office when we're on vacation."

Aaron laughs. "No, I'm not talking about taking two weeks off and going on vacation. John needs to stay at home or hang in town without going into work." Ann sighs, as if she gets the challenge. "I think that after the first two weeks, both you and John will get a sense of just how much work you two have if you're going to be ready to leave the company. In fact, I'd be surprised if you don't both come away from the experience with some major questions about the wisdom of John completely retiring."

John frowns. "I'm not sure why you'd say that. I mean, two weeks isn't a very long time."

Aaron answers. "No, it's not. But you'd be surprised how long it feels. The first couple of days will be fine. After a week, you'll be chomping at the bit to come back in. Everything in you will want to do that. But you can't. Those are the rules. If you do, you'll have to start all over again in a couple of weeks. You need to experience what not being at Aardvark is going to be like."

The old John comes back. "You have no idea what you're talking about. This is going to be a piece of cake."

Aaron expects this reaction from John. It's the first time he's really pushed back on an idea during this trip. "Let me ask you a question. When was the last time you spent more than four days away from Aardvark, when you weren't sick or out of town?"

Ann laughs. "I can answer that. Never."

"That's my point. Going on vacation and traveling is fun. You'll do plenty of that when you retire. You're also going to be spending way more time at home. This is a tough transition, one that almost all my clients fail the first time they try. I'm willing to bet that John won't make the two weeks away and will have to start over again at least once or twice."

John winces. "You don't have much faith in me do you?"

"This has nothing to do with how much faith I have in you. I've seen it over and over again. You've spent almost forty years obsessing about your business on a daily basis. You've found reasons to come in even on a Saturday or Sunday. Just to check on this thing or that thing. It's hard to change gears and not come in, for everyone. Trust me, the same held true for me once."

John shrugs. "Well, let's talk about calls. How am I supposed to keep track of what's going on here if I can't call in?"

Ann interrupts her husband "What's going to happen here in two weeks that could put the company at risk? If there's a fire, you'll hear about it."

John shrugs. Aaron jumps in. "First-generation business owners often have a constant paranoia thing. That's what kept you alive. And it's hard to let go of. That's part of our job now, to unhook you from that need to keep an eye on everything."

Aaron rests his elbows on his knees and focuses on John. "You'll still have access to your dashboards. If any of the numbers fall out, which is highly unlikely, then you're allowed to come in. Does that sound fair?" John nods. "That also means you failed the two-week test and will have to start over.

"When you successfully pass this test, the next quarter, you'll do it all over again. This time, instead of two weeks, we're going to go for three weeks. Then, sometime in the six months that follow, you'll do four weeks." Aaron observes the horrified look on John's face but carries on nonetheless. "If you're like the others who've done this exercise, you're going to find that three weeks is twice as hard as two weeks and a full month is almost impossible. Most people never make the four weeks, at least, not the first time they try."

Ann says, "I'm not sure I like this experiment. I've not had any time to plan. I mean, how am I going to be able to handle having John around that much? Sure, I'd love to eat breakfast with him every morning…" Her voice trails off. "I'm not sure having him just hanging around the house is a great idea. What's he going to do with all of that time? Take up bridge?"

Aaron smiles. "That's the whole point of this exercise. Over the next year or eighteen months, you'll both experience what it'll be like when John leaves the company. It's going to be a big adjustment for both of you. The good news is these first go-rounds are practice. You'll get a chance to test what works and what doesn't. You'll have time to make the kind of changes in both of your lives that will allow you to live together in a different way, to make the necessary accommodations."

Both Ann and John look nervous. Aaron expects this reaction.

John thinks this should be easy, but he's not sure why he's feeling so unnerved. So much for the work with Aaron being easier this go-round!

"You know," John says, "every time you come here, you seem to drop a bombshell on me just before you leave. It really annoys the heck out of me. What's up with that?"

Aaron spreads his palms open. "If I had this conversation with you when I first got here, or even before now, you likely would have rejected my suggestion out of hand. On top of that, Ann needed the chance to integrate the information we've gone over, or none of this would have made any sense. It just seems like I'm springing the hard stuff on you at the end.

"You've got some interesting challenges ahead of you—the one you share with Ann being the biggest. Everything we're asking of the people in the company is minor compared to what you two are going to experience. At the end of the day, that's just the way it is."

John shrugs. "Well, that's comforting," he says sarcastically.

"One more thing. When you're doing your two-week, then three- and four-week sabbaticals, it doesn't count if you help Adam buy a company. If you have to take time away from Aardvark to do that, we'll label that as work. If you depend on working with Adam to occupy your time and attention, you'll be setting yourself up for a fall."

Ann says, "True. Anyway, Adam isn't interested in having his father involved. If your relationship is ever going to improve, you need to give it space and time."

Aaron gets up. "It's time for me to go." He reaches out and shakes both John and Ann's hands. "Thanks so much for your hospitality. I'm looking forward to seeing both of you soon. John, you have my number, call me any time you need. I'm always honored when I'm allowed to do this type of work with a family like yours. It's a real pleasure."

With that Aaron leaves the office, closing the door quietly behind him.

John turns to Ann. "Well, what do you think?"

Ann answers, "I like the plan. But I've got to admit I'm not so sure about having you around the house all day. I'm looking forward to it and am scared of it, all at the same time." She pauses. "I really hope it works out for Adam. Last night he called, and for the first time in years, he sounded genuinely excited. This could be such an exciting time for us all."

"I agree," John says, grabbing Ann's hand and guiding her toward the door. "How about you and I grab some lunch? My treat."

ACKNOWLEDGMENTS

There's a saying that it takes a village to raise a child. I would add to that; it takes a village to write a book.

First, I want to thank my content editor, Ann Sheybani. This is the second book we've done together. Without her patience and guidance, this book would be a raging mess. She's taught me more about writing during both of our book projects than all of my English teachers combined.

Second, I want to thank Sissi Haner for her fine line editing. Without her work, you would see grammatical errors that would make you grind your teeth. Her work saved you from having to do this.

I also want to thank the team at Morgan James Publishing. Karen Anderson and her team have done a phenomenal job at keeping our process moving forward and providing much needed guidance in improving this book.

There are three people who have generously shared their wisdom and teaching that shows up in the book.

Susan Bradley, from Sudden Money and the Financial Transitionist Institute, is the developer of the stages of transition that play a major role in the planning that John and his wife, Ann, go through as they think about the next stage of their life. This tool is one of many that those who are Certified Financial Transitionists® (CeFT) learn about as they go through her program. Susan is not only a brilliant teacher but a great friend. I'm indebted to her and am happy to call her a friend.

I first learned of John Brown, founder of Business Enterprise Institute, in 1997 through his book *How to Run Your Business So You Can Leave It in Style*. Shortly after, I took part in one of his early boot camps, where I learned the technical side of private business succession planning. He is a good friend, and, over the years, we've shared many meals and had intense discussions about what it means for a business owner to transition from their business to whatever is next in their life. His guidance has been and is most helpful.

The framework of John's book is around his seven steps, and I've added an eighth one. Frameworks are most useful when planning and creating fast actions. When you know what to do and why it's important, adding who you need to help and the actual steps become easy.

The third is Mike Michalowicz and his book *Profit First*. The four buckets of profit are a direct outgrowth of working with Mike on how Profit First works.

If you're an advisor, I recommend you look at all three and consider whether any of them fit into your practice.

If you're a business owner, find an advisor who has had training in each of these disciplines and see how they can help you get your company to be sale ready.

Finally, I want to thank all of those who have been early readers and provided comments along the way. The most important of this group is my wife, Suzanne Kneller. She not only provided wonderful comments, she gave me the space and support to write this book. The rest who have been early readers know who they are, and I truly appreciate your help and support.

Enjoy this book. It's been a labor of love.

ABOUT THE AUTHOR

Josh Patrick is a serial entrepreneur. He's been fascinated by business since he was seven years old and sold candy to other neighborhood kids.

He is the author of *Sustainable: A Fable About Creating a Personally and Economically Sustainable Business*. He's been a blogger for "You're the Boss" at *The New York Times*, been a columnist for *The Huffington Post*, Forbes.com and Inc.com.

He's been reading a book once a week since he was a junior in college forty-six years ago, and over 75% of his reading has been about what it takes for a private business to be successful and, ultimately, sustainable.

He began his first "real" business right after he graduated from Boston University. He started with one part-time employee and grew that business to one that had ninety employees.

He's held leadership positions with several trade associations and has been on founding boards for several arts organizations in the Burlington, Vermont, area. As Chairperson of the Education Committee for the National Vending Association, Josh taught and developed courses on people management, operations management, and financial management. All three lead to a company that is economically sustainable and, ultimately, sale ready.

In his free time, he loves to read, listen to music (especially jam bands like the Grateful Dead), ride his bike, ski, and pet his dogs. He lives in Northern Vermont with his wife, Suzanne, and his two Golden Retrievers, Cassady and Barlow.

He is most appreciative of you reading this book and hopes you walk away with a better understanding of the steps needed to create a Sale Ready Business.

You can find Josh at jpatrick@stage2planning.com or by visiting one of his three websites.

- **SaleReadyCompany.com:** Extra information on creating a sale ready company
- **Stage2Planning.com:** Financial planning information
- **SustainableBusiness.co:** Podcast and videos on creating a sale ready company

READING LIST

This is a partial list of books I recommend for all business owners. Many of these are cited in the text of the book. If you have books you think should be added, just email me at jpatrick@stage2planning.com and let me know what I missed.

These books are not listed in any particular order. I have grouped them by subject. Must-Read books are listed twice, once under the topic heading Must-Read Books, and the second is by specific topic. The must-read books are where I would start first.

Must-Read Books

Brown, Steve. *The Golden Toilet: Stop Flushing Your Marketing Budget into Your Website and Build a System That Grows Your Business.* ROI Publishing 2020.

Dixon, Matthew, Brent Adamson. *The Challenger Sale: Taking Control of the Customer Conversation.* Portfolio, 2011.

Drucker, Peter F. *Management: Tasks, Responsibilities, Practices.* Harper Business, 1985.

Farber, Steve. *The Radical Leap: A Personal Lesson in Extreme Leadership*. Dearborn Trade, 2004.

Fuller, Buckminster, R. *Critical Path*. St. Martin's Griffin, 1981.

Goldratt, Eliyahu M., Jeff Cox. *The Goal: A Process of Ongoing Improvement*. North River Press, 1984.

Lencioni, Patrick. *The Advantage: Why Organizational Health Trumps Everything Else in Business*. Jossey-Bass, 2012.

Michalowicz, Mike. *Fix This Next: Make the Vital Change That Will Level Up Your Business*. Portfolio, 2020.

Michalowicz, Mike. *Profit First: A Simple System to Transform Any Business from a Cash-Eating Monster to a Money-Making Machine*. Obsidian Press, 2014.

Miller, Donald. *Building a StoryBrand: Clarify Your Message So Customers Will Listen*. Harper Collins Leadership, 2017.

Night, Phil. *Shoe Dog: A Memoir by the Creator of Nike*. Scribner 2016.

Port, Michael. *Book Yourself Solid Illustrated: The Fastest, Easiest, and Most Reliable System for Getting More Clients Than You Can Handle Even If You Hate Marketing and Selling*. Wiley, 2006.

Rhimes, Shonda. *Year of Yes: How to Dance It Out, Stand in the Sun and Be Your Own Person*. Simon & Schuster, 2015.

Sutherland, Jeff. *Scrum: The Art of Doing Twice the Work in Half the Time*. Crown Business, 2014.

Westover, Tara. *Educated: A Memoir.* Random House, 2018.

Wickman, Gino. *Traction: Get a Grip on Your Business.* Smashwords, Inc., 2007.

Management

Brodsky, Norm, Bo Burlingham. *The Knack: How Street-Smart Entrepreneurs Learn to Handle Whatever Comes Up.* Portfolio Hardcover, 2008.

Buckingham, Marcus, Curt Coffman. *First, Break All the Rules: What the World's Greatest Managers Do Differently.* Gallup Press, 1998.

Collins, James C., Morten T. Hansen. *Great by Choice: Uncertainty, Chaos, and Luck—Why Some Thrive Despite Them All.* Harper Business, 2011.

Conley, Chip. *Wisdom at Work: The Making of a Modern Elder.* Currency, 2018.

Covey, Stephen M.R. *The Speed of Trust: The One Thing that Changes Everything.* Free Press, 2006.

Drucker, Peter F. *The Effective Executive: The Definitive guide to Getting the Right Things Done.* Harper Business, 1966.

Drucker, Peter F. *The Essential Drucker.* Regan Books, 2000.

Drucker. Peter F. *Management: Tasks, Responsibilities, Practices.* Harper Business, 1985.

Duhigg, Charles. *Smarter Faster Better: The Secrets of Being Productive in Life and Business.* Random House, 2016.

Harnish, Verne. *Scaling UP: How a Few Companies Make It....and Why the Rest Don't.* Gazelles Inc., 2014.

Lencioni, Patrick. *The Advantage: Why Organizational Health Trumps Everything Else in Business.* Jossey-Bass, 2012.

Mackey, John E., Rajendra S. Sisodia. *Conscious Capitalism: Liberating the Heroic Spirit of Business.* Harvard Business Review Press, 2013.

Michalowicz, Mike. *Fix This Next: Make the Vital Change That Will Level Up Your Business.* Portfolio, 2020.

Michalowicz, Mike. *Profit First: A Simple System to Transform Any Business from a Cash-Eating Monster to a Money-Making Machine.* Obsidian Press, 2014.

Pink, Daniel H. *Drive, The Surprising Truth About What Motivates Us.* Riverhead Books, 2009.

Wickman, Gino, Mark C. Winters. *Rocket Fuel: The One Essential Combination That Will Get You More of What You Want from Your Business.* BenBella Books, 2015.

Wickman, Gino. *Traction: Get a Grip on Your Business.* Smashwords, Inc., 2007.

Marketing

Baer, Jay. *Hug Your Haters: How to Embrace Complaints and Keep Your Customers.* Portfolio, 2016.

Brown, Steve. *The Golden Toilet: Stop Flushing Your Marketing Budget into Your Website and Build A System That Grows Your Business.* ROI Publishing 2020.

Dooley, Roger. *Brainfluence: 100 Ways to Persuade and Convince Consumers with Neuromarketing*. John Wiley and Sons, 2011.

Gordon, Steve. *Unstoppable Referrals: 10X Referrals Half the Effort*. Unstoppable CEO Press, 2014.

Holiday, Ryan. *Perennial Seller: The Art of Making and Marketing Work That Lasts*. Portfolio, 2017.

Levesque, Ryan. *Ask: The Counterintuitive Online Formula to Discover Exactly What Your Customers Want to Buy… Create a Mass of Raving Fans… and Take Any Business to the Next Level*. Dunham Books, 2015.

Levesque, Ryan. *Choose: The Single Most Important Decision Before Starting Your Business*. Hay House Books 2019.

Marshall, Perry. *80/20 Sales and Marketing: The Definitive Guide to Working Less and Making More*. Entrepreneur Press, 2013.

Michalowicz, Mike. *Surge: Time the Marketplace, Ride the Wave of Consumer Demand, and Become Your Industry's Big Kahuna*. Obsidian Press, 2016.

Miller, Donald. *Building a StoryBrand: Clarify Your Message So Customers Will Listen*. Harper Collins Leadership, 2017.

Miller, Donald. *Marketing Made Simple: A Step-by-Step StoryBrand Guide for Any Business*. HarperCollins Leadership, 2020.

Port, Michael. *Book Yourself Solid Illustrated: The Fastest, Easiest, and Most Reliable System for Getting More Clients Than You Can Handle Even If You Hate Marketing and Selling*. Wiley, 2006.

Family Business

Jay, Meg. *The Defining Decade: Why Your Twenties Matter—And How to Make the Most of Them Now.* Twelve, 2012.

Kolbe, Kathy, Amy Bruske. *Business is Business: Reality Checks for Family-Owned Companies.* Greenleaf Book Group Press, 2017.

Pullen, Courtney. *Intentional Wealth: How Families build Legacies of Stewardship and Financial Health.* CreateSpace, 2013.

Sales

Adamson, Brent, Matthew Dixon, Pet Spenner, Nick Toman. *The Challenger Customer: Selling to the Hidden Influencer Who Can Multiply Your Results.* Portfolio, 2015.

Beckwith, Harry. *Selling the Invisible: A Field Guide to Modern Marketing.* Warner Books, 1997.

Dixon, Matthew, Brent Adamson. *The Challenger Sale: Taking Control of the Customer Conversation.* Portfolio, 2011.

MacKay, Harvey. *Swim with the Sharks Without Being Eaten Alive: Outsell, Outmanage, Outmotivate, and Outnegotiate your Competition.* Harper Business, 1988.

Pink, Daniel H. *To Sell is Human: The Surprising Truth About Persuading, Convincing, and Influencing Others.* Canongate Books, 2013.

Scott, David Meerman. *The New Rules of Sales and Service: How to Use Agile Selling, Real-Time Customer*

Engagement, Big Data, Content and Storytelling to Grow Your Business. John Wiley and Sons, 2014.

Walker, Jeff. *Launch: An Internet Millionaire's Secret Formula to Sell Almost Anything Online, Build a Business You Love, and Live the Life of Your Dreams.* Morgan James Publishing, 2014.

Leadership

Covey, Stephen R. *Principle-Centered Leadership.* Fireside Press, 1991.

Epstein, David. *Range: Why Generalists Triumph in a Specialized World.* Riverhead Books, 2019.

Goldsmith, Marshall, Mark Reiter. *What Got You Here Won't Get You There: How Successful People Become Even More Successful.* Hyperion, 2007.

Kegan, Robert, Lisa Laskow Lahey. *Immunity to Change: How to Overcome It and Unlock the Potential in Yourself and Your Organization (Leadership for the Common Good).* Harvard Business Review Press, 2009.

Kouzes, James M., Barry Z. Posner. *The Leadership Challenge.* Jossey-Bass, 1987.

McChrystal, Stanley. *Team of Teams: New Rules of Engagement for a Complex World.* Portfolio, 2015.

Murthy, Vivek H. *Together: Why Social Connection Holds the Key to Better Health, Higher Performance, and Greater Happiness.* Harper Wave 2020.

Prochaska, James O., John C. Norcross, Carlo C. DiClemente. *Changing for Good: A Revolutionary Six-*

Stage Program for Overcoming Bad Habits and Moving Your Life Positively Forward. William Morrow, 1994.

Sinek, Simon. *Leaders Eat Last: Why Some Teams Pull Together and Others Don't.* Portfolio, 2013.

People Management

Colvin, Geoff. *Talent is Overrated: What Really Separates World-Class Performers from Everybody Else.* Portfolio, 2008.

Farber, Steve. *Love is Just Damn Good Business: Do What You Love in the Service of People Who Love What You Do.* McGraw-Hill Education 2019.

Goldsmith, Marshall. *Triggers: Creating Behaviors That Lasts—Becoming the Person You Want to Be.* Crown Business, 2015.

James, Aaron. *Assholes: A Theory.* Ancho, 2012.

Logan, Dave, John King, Halee Fischer-Wright. *Tribal Leadership: Leveraging Natural Groups to Build a Thriving Organization.* Harper Business, 2008.

Negotiating

Patterson, Kerry, Joseph Grenny, Ron McMillan, Al Switzler. *Crucial Conversations: Tools for Talking When Stakes Are High.* McGraw-Hill, 2001.

Voss, Chris. *Never Split the Difference: Negotiating As If Your Life Depended On It.* Harper Business, 2016.

Innovation

Christensen, Clayton M., Taddy Hall, Karen Dillon, David Duncan. *Competing Against Luck*. Harper Business, 2016.

Christensen, Clayton M., Michael E. Raynor. *The Innovator's Solution: Creating and Sustaining Successful Growth*. Harvard Business School Press, 2003.

Business Succession Planning

Brown, John H. *The Completely Revised How to Run Your Business So You Can Leave It in Style*. Business Enterprise Press, 1990.

Short, Kevin. *Sell Your Business for an Outrageous Price: An Insider's Guide to Getting More Than You Ever Thought Possible*. AMACOM/American Management Association, 2014.

Process Improvement and Systematization

Deming, W. Edwards. *Out of the Crisis*. MIT Press, 1982.

Dennis, Pascal. *The Remedy: Bringing Lean Thinking Out of the Factory to Transform the Entire Organization*. John Wiley and Sons, 2010.

Liker, Jeffrey K., Gary L. Convis. *The Toyota Way to Lean Leadership: Achieving and Sustaining Excellence Through Leadership Development*. McGraw Hill, 2011.

Sutherland, Jeff. *Scrum: The Art of Doing Twice the Work in Half the Time*. Crown Business, 2014.

Sutherland, J.J. *The Scrum Fieldbook: The Art of Changing the Possible*. Currency, 2019.

Miscellaneous

Achor, Shawn. *The Happiness Advantage: The Seven Principles of Positive Psychology That Fuel Success and Performance at Work.* Crown Business, 2010.

Airely, Dan. *Predictably Irrational: The Hidden Forces That Shape Our Decisions.* HarperCollins Canada, 2008.

Ducker, Chris. *Virtual Freedom: How to Work with Virtual Staff to Buy More Time, Become More Productive, and Build Your Dream Business.* BenBella Books, 2014.

Fuller, Buckminster, R. *Critical Path.* St. Martin's Griffin, 1981.

Grant, Adam M., *Give and Take: A Revolutionary Approach to Success.* Viking, 2013.

Holiday, Ryan. *Stillness is the Key.* Portfolio 2019.

Levitt, Steven D., Stephen J. Dubner. *Think Like a Freak.* William Morrow, 2014.

Lewis, Michael. *The Undoing Project: A Friendship That Changed Our Minds.* W.W. Norton & Company, 2016.

Newport, Cal. *Deep Work: Rules for Focused Success in a Distracted World.* Grand Central Publishing, 2016.

Patterson, Kerry, Joseph Grenny, Ron McMillan, Al Switzler. *Crucial Conversations: Tools for Talking When Stakes Are High.* McGraw Hill Education, 2002.

Pine II, B. Joseph, James H. Gilmore. *The Experience Economy: Work is Theatre & Every Business a Stage.* Harvard Business Review Press, 1999.

Port, Michael. *Steal the Show: From Speeches to Job Interviews to Deal-Closing Pitches, How to Guarantee a*

Standing Ovation for All the Performances in Your Life. Houghton Mifflin, Harcourt, 2015.

Slee, Rob. *Time Really Is Money: How To Work For $5,000 Per Hour.* Burn the Boat Press, 2015.

Thaler, Richard H., *Misbehaving: The Making of Behavioral Economics.* W.W. Norton Company, 2015.

Tugend, Alina. *Better by Mistake: The Unexpected Benefits of Being Wrong.* Riverhead Books, 2011.

Business Fables

Coelho, Paulo, Alan R. Clarke. *The Alchemist.* HarperCollins, 1993.

Farber, Steve, Matthew Kelly. *Greater Than Yourself: The Ultimate Lesson of True Leadership.* Crown Business, 2009.

Farber, Steve. *The Radical Leap: A Personal Lesson in Extreme Leadership.* Dearborn Trade, 2004.

Goldratt, Eliyahu M., Jeff Cox. *The Goal: A Process of Ongoing Improvement.* North River Press, 1984.

Lencioni, Patrick. *Getting Naked: A Business Fable about Shedding the Three Fears That Sabotage Client Loyalty.* Jossey-Bass, 2002.

Lencioni, Patrick. *The Five Dysfunctions of a Team: A Leadership Fable.* Jossey-Bass, 2002.

Lencioni, Patrick. *The Ideal Team Player: How To Recognize and Cultivate the Three Essential Virtues.* Jossey-Bass, 2016.

The Arbinger Institute. *The Anatomy of Peace: Resolving the Heart of Conflict.* Barrett-Koehler Publishers 2015.

The Arbinger Institute. *Leadership and Self-Deception: Getting Out of the Box*. Barrett-Kohler Publishers, 2018.

Wickman, Gino, Mike Paton. *Get A Grip: An Entrepreneurial Fable... Your Journey to Get Real, Get Simple, and Get Results*. BenBella Books, 2012.

Memoirs and Biography

Branson, Richard. *The Virgin Way: Everything I Know About Leadership*. Portfolio, 2014.

Catmull, Ed, Amy Wallace. *Creativity, Inc.: Overcoming the Unseen Forces That Stand in the Way of True Inspiration*. Random House, 2014.

Hsieh, Tony. *Delivering Happiness: A Path to Profits, Passions and Purpose*. Grand Central Publishing, 2010.

Iger, Robert. *The Ride of a Lifetime: Lessons Learned from 15 Years as CEO of the Walt Disney Company*. Random House, 2019.

Levy, Steven. *In the Plex: How Google Thinks, Works, and Shapes Our Lives*. Simon & Schuster, 2011.

Night, Phil. *Shoe Dog: A Memoir by the Creator of Nike*. Scribner 2016.

Price, David A. *The Pixar Touch: The Making of a Company*. Knopf, 2008.

Rhimes, Shonda. *The Year of Yes: How to Dance It Out, Stand In the Sun and Be Your Own Person*. Simon & Schuster, 2015.

Schultz, Howard, Joanne Gordon. *Onward: How Starbucks Fought For Its Life without Losing Its Soul.* Rodale Books, 2011.

Vance, Ashlee. *Elon Musk: Tesla, SpaceX, and the Quest for a Fantastic Future,.* Ecco 2015.

Westover, Tara. *Educated.* Random House, 2018.

Get Your Free Bonus Material!

Thank you for reading our parable *The Sale Ready Company,* where you found tools and strategies John, his family, and his company used to create a sale ready company and get his business ready for the next owners.

As an additional thank you for reading this book, I've created a special section of checklists, infographics, and ebooks on strategies that *never made it into the book*!

- ✔ The stages of transition John will go through.
- ✔ The 8 steps to create a sale ready company.
- ✔ The two sides of money.
- ✔ How to hire for unique abilities.
- ✔ 7 family business secrets you need to know.
- ✔ Business relationships and roles in your business.
- ✔ And much, much more!

SaleReadyCompany.com/bonus

Join our Free Online Community!

If you're interested in creating a sale ready company (but not in selling) visit us at **SaleReadyCompany.com**.

Share your experiences and challenges as you create a sale ready company for your business. And, remember, a sale ready company has little to nothing to do with selling your company. It just means you've created a company that someone else would want to own!

 Visit **SaleReadyCompany.com/bonus** to get your free bonus materials.